SANA
JAYASURIYA

Chandresh Narayanan is a senior cricket writer and has written for various publications like *The Times of India,* Cricketniravana.com and *The Indian Express.*

Narayanan also worked as the content head of the official website of the Indian Premier League (IPL) and the media and communications officer at the International Cricket Council (ICC).

He lives in Mumbai.

SANATH JAYASURIYA

A Biography

CHANDRESH NARAYANAN

RUPA

Published by
Rupa Publications India Pvt. Ltd 2019
7/16, Ansari Road, Daryaganj
New Delhi 110002

Sales centres:
Allahabad Bengaluru Chennai
Hyderabad Jaipur Kathmandu
Kolkata Mumbai

ISBN: 978-93-5333-358-4

First impression 2019

10 9 8 7 6 5 4 3 2 1

The moral right of the author has been asserted.

Printed at Nutech Print Services, Faridabad

I would like to dedicate this effort to my parents (Narayanan and Usha), my sister (Kanchana) and my wife (Sangeeta).

Contents

That Cyclone Sanath

By Renuka

T'was a humid day in Singapore,
On the fine old green grass Padang,
And the Singer Cup got off,
To a damn explosive bang.

It was Pakistan/Sri Lanka,
The Lankans batting first,
And out came the dynamic duo,
One with a craving thirst.

Cyclone Sanath turned around to his mate,
The great Lightning Kalu,
And said, 'Today will be our day',
Let's smash an old record or two.

Sanath Jayasuriya

The great Waqar Younis ran in to bowl,
And pitched too short for one,
And Cyclone pulled it to the fence,
An omen of things to come.

Like a cat amongst the pigeons,
Sanath smote them true and well,
And tore up the opening bowlers,
Like a demon out of hell.
The Singaporeans were quite impressed,
At the blazing batting blitz,
'We thought cricket a boring game,
Played by old crusty Brits'.

They said 'marvellous' in Mandarin
And 'crikes' in Cantonese,
In Tamil they said, 'Terrific!',
And in Malay they said, 'More Please!'

'Cyclone Sanath's not bad lah!'
They said in Singlish too,
And on the field a few other words,
Were muttered in Urdu.
Captain Sohail was not impressed,
At his team feeling so small,
'You strike bowlers are useless,'
Give me that bloody ball,'
He rubbed it on his jock strap,
And kissed his lucky clover,
Then bowled a group of six balls,

That Cyclone Sanath By Renuka

That redefined the word 'over'.
The first went over the car park,
The second over the CBD,
The third went towards Malaysia,
At the speed of sound times three.

The Singapore government was in panic,
'Quick, someone ring Johore,
Before our good neighbours think,
That we're trying to start a war'.

The fourth flew right up in the air,
Then dive-bombed the town too,
Creating the greatest airborne panic,
Since Nineteen Forty Two.

At Raffles they ran for shelter,
They covered their heads at Boat Quay,
And even the frightened Merlion squeaked,
'How about a helmet and pads for me?'

Twenty-nine runs off the first over,
And poor Sohail gave right up,
And was heard muttering a couple of words,
That rhymed with 'Brother Duck'.

But the locals just loved it,
As they saw the fastest ton ever.
Even old Uncle Lee Kwan Yew,
Said, 'Crips this lad is clever'.

Sanath Jayasuriya

'Let's offer him a new job,
Down at Changi Prison farm.
If he can strike like that with a bat
What could he do with a rotan?'

But in Karachi they were crying,
And bawling in Lahore.
'Hockey and squash aren't bad games,
Isn't cricket such a bore?'

In Balochistan and Punjab,
And the NW Frontier too,
They said, 'We haven't felt so helpless
Since Alexander marched right through'.

And in Benazir's cabinet room,
She told her generals, 'Listen,
This country doesn't need nukes,
It needs a Cyclone protection system!'

And finally, they got Cyclone out,
For a score of 130,
11 sixes, 11 fours,
Balls faced: just 63!

The score ended at 349,
And Waqar picked up four scalps,
But looking at a score like that,
The batsman just said, 'Yelp!'

That Cyclone Sanath By Renuka

The Pakistanis batted bravely,
And lost by 30 runs.
But of all the innings played that day,
We'll remember just one.

And in the ancient lands of Pakistan,
Some names will always be spoken with fear,
Like Tamerlane the Terrible,
And Sanath Jayasuriya.

PS:
In the parks and street of Singapore,
That clean, green fine city.
You'll see a lot of red circle signs,
Saying what you cannot do or be.

Like jaywalking or littering
That are against the Singapore way,
Or spitting, chewing gums, or breaking plants,
Or trying your laces the wrong way.

Well they're putting a new sign up now,
Inside those circles red,
Of a slightly balding cricketer,
Two huge sideburns frame his head.

They're saying, 'We like the game of cricket,
We give 10 marks out of 10,
But if Cyclone Sanath's at the crease,
No way is Sohail bowling again!'

Introduction

Sri Lanka's cricket history has always been about fighting above their weight on the big stage. When Sri Lanka's batsmen Sunil Wettimuny and Duleep Mendis were destroyed by thunderbolts of Australia's typhoon Jeff Thomson during the 1975 World Cup, it was a landmark moment in cricket. Even though the bouncers rendered the batsmen unfit, Sri Lanka fought fire with fire quite valiantly.

Sri Lanka's cricket team has always had some of the most attractive batsmen. These batsmen can kill the opposition with their elegance. The 1970s was about the tenacious lot led by Mendis, Bandula Warnapura and Anura Tennekoon. They used to have regular exchanges with India in unofficial Tests, especially with the Tamil Nadu Ranji Trophy team in the now defunct M.J. Gopalan Trophy. This helped the Sri Lankan team cut their teeth on the world stage as they gained immense experience. They were one of the most promising non-Test playing sides in the world. Indian fans still cannot forget the 'humiliation' of losing to Sri Lanka in the 1979 World Cup.

But it was not until 1981 when Sri Lanka was awarded the Test status for its consistent performances in limited-overs cricket that they actually came into their own. The era of the 1980s was the time Sri Lanka's batting came of age. It was marked by the arrival of Roy Dias, followed by Aravinda de Silva, along with Roshan Mahanama. Cricket watchers in Sri Lanka still speak with awe about de Silva's batting prowess. They cannot get over the fact that he hooked India's legendary Kapil Dev off the very first ball of an innings in a Test match at Colombo in 1985–86.

With this, the era in which Sri Lanka would compete with aplomb, at least at home, began. But there was also the issue of umpiring in their home matches. International captains like Imran Khan and Kapil had a problem with the same and came away bitter from their experience in Sri Lanka in the 1980s. Sri Lankan cricket was just about afloat throughout the 1980s. They had the odd win away from home against the much-fancied sides, but they were not consistent. For a sport struggling to find six competent sides, this was hardly the way to go forward.

The Sri Lankan cricket—and the sport on the world stage—needed a spark. There was hardly an indication of that happening, until 1989, when Sri Lanka introduced an unassuming youngster. Only twenty then, he had not proved to the world that he was going to change the game in a few years.

Sanath Teran Jayasuriya was a young village boy at the time—someone who quickly climbed the ladder via the age-group structure. The retirement of a number of seniors, especially the likes of Mendis—then Ranjan Madugalle—necessitated the initiation of some fresh blood into the system. Sanath was meant to be an all-rounder who batted usefully in the middle-order. He may as well have ended up as one of the many journeymen cricketers who ply their trade very quietly. However, his fielding—thanks to his amazing fitness level owing to years of playing on the beachfront of Matara—was a clinching factor. In the initial couple of years, it was his razor-sharp fielding that caught everyone's attention.

Despite this, his name remained one of the most difficult to pronounce in the Sri Lankan team since the late 1980s. His first real performance came in a One-Day International (ODI) against England at Moratuwa in 1993. But it was still not enough for the world to sit up and notice.

He was finally noticed in the 1994–95 season when he made the opening position in the shorter format his own. He was now being let loose against rivals. But even then, he had not been fully recognized. However, in just twelve months, Sanath's, and subsequently Sri Lanka's, fortune turned. The spark that world cricket had been looking for was finally spotted. It was in the wrists of the man they all claimed climbed coconut trees for fun. Those iron wrists generated so much power that the world began to tremble in fear. They were first unveiled in Australia just before the 1996 World Cup. Then came the showpiece event. The sight of Phil Defreitas and Manoj Prabhakar, both adequate ODI bowlers, looking dazed is something no one will ever forget.

Sanath proved to be impressive from the very first ball, with an equally dynamic partner in wicketkeeper Romesh Kaluwitharana. Sri Lanka had the experience of Asanka Gurusinha, de Silva, Hashan Tillakaratne and Mahanama. Above all, there was the general of them all—Arjuna Ranatunga. It was he who gave permission to proceed with this strategy and from there on, there was no looking back. Sanath's destructive batting and his fast accurate left-arm spin and fielding made for a true winner. On top of that, Sri Lanka's ever-improving side acquired a couple of more important weapons in the magical spinner Muttiah Muralitharan and the consistent pacer Chaminda Vaas.

These factors ensured that Sri Lanka's cricket had turned a corner forever. There were a few bumps on the way with change in personnel, loss of form and of course the disaster of the 1999 World Cup. But it was then down to the man who had initiated the first renaissance, Sanath, to lead Sri Lanka to the second one as well—only this time from the front as a leader.

Leadership sat well with Sanath as Sri Lanka's fortunes in Test cricket turned for the better. The team became an all-rounder, with Sanath contributing heavily both on and off the field. The good run continued till the 2003 World Cup. But once they lost that, it was clear that Sanath would not overstay his welcome as the captain.

Everyone felt Sanath would apply this clarity of approach to his own cricketing career. There were times after he stepped down as captain when it was felt he could pull the stumps on his time on the field. But he battled on and came back stronger. However, he reached an age where his form in every match was scrutinized. He need not have stretched himself beyond a point. He retired once from Test cricket, and then made a dramatic comeback, only to be pushed into exiting soon.

In the phase between 2008 and 2011, he was superfluous to the requirement of the team. This was quite a change from his heydays in the mid-1990s when he had been essential for Sri Lanka's good fortune. Then there were also the allegations of political interference to engineer his re-entry into the national side because he had taken a political plunge at the time. Did this tar Sanath's legacy? Well, according to his critics, it may well have because since then, he was viewed quite differently. His final hurrah after crossing forty was indeed a sad commentary on the way his career panned out towards the end.

Sanath's life after his cricketing days has been equally dramatic, especially his days as a minister in the government of Sri Lanka. He found real-time politicking quite a challenge, but in his stint as the chairman of selectors, Sanath may well have found similarities between cricket and politics.

Politics and cricket are intertwined in Sri Lanka. No one understood this better than Sanath. He made a good fist of it for a while, but the noose was tightening with time. He finally gave in and ended his long association with Sri Lankan cricket for good—or at least that is what it seems.

Along the way, Sanath has made many friends, but also has numerous adversaries. He has touched many lives in Sri Lanka with his batting, but many people also feel that he overstayed his welcome. Whatever the verdict is on Sanath the man, there is one unanimous verdict on Sanath the cricketer—there simply was no one like him.

He changed the face of Sri Lanka and world cricket. His cricketing achievements do not quite tell the full story of his impact on the cricket field. He was the 'Matara Mauler' who was meant to not fade away swiftly but shine brightly as he did for 23 years.

1

Modest Beginnings

Matara is about 160 kilometres away from the capital of Colombo and is on the southernmost tip of Sri Lanka. Several foreign rulers have eyed the town since the fifteenth century. While the Portuguese ruled Matara in the sixteenth century, the Dutch took over in the eighteenth century. Late in the eighteenth century, the Dutch handed over the strategically significant Matara to the British.

Today, Matara is a city that has extensive Dutch and British architecture. The lighthouse at Dondra Head, built by the Dutch, is considered one of the most beautiful architectural wonders in Sri Lanka. The Matara Fort and Star Fort, also built by the Dutch, continue to attract tourists in huge numbers. Matara Bodhiya, a Buddhist temple and the site of a sacred fig tree, is also a popular tourist hub. The majority of the town's population practise Buddhism. The other big attraction of Matara is its beach.

Tucked away in a corner of Matara is a tiny hamlet of Kotuwegoda. Here, just a stone's throw away from the Kotuwegoda beach, in July of 1969, someone was born—someone who would outshine all the invaders or rulers who had raised their flags in the city.

In a house on 45 Penny Quick Lane, as it was known then, Breeda and Dunstan Jayasuriya became proud parents of their second son, Sanath. The lane has now been renamed Mahamaya Mawatha, but the town once carried a signboard which said, 'Welcome to Sanath Country'. This was the impact he would leave in the years to come.

Sanath's father Dunstan worked as an inspector in the health department of the Matara Council, while his mother Breeda worked as a salesperson at a souvenir shop at Loksala in Galle, involving 41-kilometre travel every day. Both were devout Buddhists and they passed on the same devotion to their sons as well.

Sanath's elder brother, Chandana, took up a job in the government department. But the tiniest member of the family was only too keen to play cricket with his friends in the by-lanes. This often proved to be a nuisance as since the age of nine, he had started exhibiting his prowess at striking sixes. These shots would land in the neighbouring temple premises, causing a lot of commotion. The temple priests 'tolerated' the shots but coming from a devout Buddhist family meant that his mother disapproved of them. Little did she know that this irritating ability of her son would prove to be the turning point for her country's fortune.

Padding Up for the First Time

Tired of Sanath's cricketing antics, Breeda sent Sanath to St. Servatius College to study and play cricket. St. Servatius

College was a Catholic school and was built by British priests in 1897. Bishop of Galle, Joseph Van Reeth, was one of its earliest founders. At the beginning, the college had only 5 students, but by 1898, the number increased to 54 students. A new structure of the college was built with the help of funds that came from St. Servatius Jesuit school of Liège, Belgium. As a result, the school in Matara adopted the name of its saint, St. Servatius—a fourth-century Belgian missionary. In 1961, the Sri Lankan government took over the administration of the institution, though the Catholic priests continued supervising the education until 1965.

One of the earliest attractions of studying at St. Servatius College was its annual cricket match against rival St. Thomas College. This match has been played since 1900 and is the second-oldest cricket contest in Sri Lanka. It is also known as the Battle of the Blues or the Battle of Ruhuna. Since its centenary year in 2000, it is being played as a three-day game.

Sanath was to captain St. Servatius in 1988, while his three maternal uncles had played this annual contest in the past.

But when he first joined the institution as a nine-year-old, the college was still toying with the idea of forming an Under-11 side. The coach at the time, Lionel Wagasinghe, also an alumnus of the college, decided to pursue Principal G.A. Galappaththi to start both Under-11 and Under-13 sides.

At the age of nine, Sanath was hardly as tall as a bat and sometimes walked out to play wearing oversized second-hand pads. As a result, it became a habit for him to adjust his pads. This habit turned into a superstition over the years as he moved to international cricket.

'I touch a spot on my helmet and both my pads before every ball. And after hitting a four or a six, I have a habit of going to

3

the middle of the pitch and tapping it,' Sanath explained his superstitions.[1] In later years, his teammates joked about some of his other quirks, like getting the team's coach, Tom Moody, to adjust his bat's grip just before he stepped out to bat or getting a newcomer like Farveez Maharoof to give him throwdowns. All this, he believed, added to his good luck and resulted in good scores— and it worked too!

In many ways, these quirks were also a result of living in limited financial conditions. Sanath did not own a bat until he was eighteen. 'I used to pick one from the school bag,' he told ESPNcricinfo. 'There would be four or five in there and, if you opened like I did most of the time, you could have first pick. When I got out, I would often hand it to the new guy when we crossed.' [2]

One of the people to have received this bat during Sanath's schooldays, Ruchira Palliyagaru, is connected to the game till today. Little did anyone know then that he would turn out to be an international umpire.

In his early years, the coach, Wagasinghe, left an indelible imprint on Sanath's career. 'It was my norm to be always well-disciplined and be mentally tough at any situation. That was how I carried my school to the topmost division at junior level and produced players like Sanath and Ruchira (Palliyaguru),' said Wagasinghe.[3]

Despite his excellence in sports, Sanath did not have much

---

[1]In an interview with ESPNcricinfo, http://www.espncricinfo.com/magazine/content/story/441258.html-CN, 27 December 2009.

[2]Richard Hobson, 'The Apologetic Assassin', http://www.espncricinfo.com/wisdencricketer/content/story/321846.html, December 2007.

[3]Revata S. Silva, 'Jayasuriya: Charisma Wasted?', http://www.island.lk/2009/02/05/sports15.html

interest in academics. *Mid-Day* travelled to Matara in 2008 and reported about his commerce teacher in XII grade, Ajwad Ikram. Ikram mentioned an incident when Sanath had turned up late for a class and Ikram had promptly asked him to leave. 'I told him two things that can happen if he concentrates on cricket: if he succeeds, he would travel to foreign countries to play, but if he fails, he would end up at the culvert outside the school,' he said.[4]

Ikram's words proved prophetic.

Sanath won the award for best batsman and best all-rounder at the school level in Sri Lanka in 1988. School cricket or age-group cricket is the lifeline of cricket at the highest level in Sri Lanka. A performer in this age bracket immediately gets noticed. So, it was not a surprise when Sanath's exploits at school-level cricket achieved national acclaim.

Taking Fresh Guard

At the end of 1988, Sanath reached another high when he was picked as part of the national Under-19 side for the inaugural Under-19 Cricket World Cup in Australia. Before he left for the World Cup, his schoolmates got together to generously contribute funds for him to take to Australia as pocket money. It was a gesture that touched Sanath's heart.

Apart from Sanath, the inaugural tournament featured a number of future international captains, including Michael Atherton, Nasser Hussain (England), Lee Germon (New Zealand), Inzamam-ul-Haq

---

[4]'Walking Down Sanath's Street', Sanath Jayasuriya Blogspot, http://sanath189.blogspot.com/2008/09/walking-down-sanaths-street-brief-tour.html, 26 September 2008.

(Pakistan) and Brian Lara, Jimmy Adams and Ridley Jacobs (West Indies).

Other notable players included Mark Ramprakash (England), Aminul Islam (Bangladesh), Narendra Hirwani (India) and Mushtaq Ahmed, Basit Ali and Aqib Javed (Pakistan). Along with Sanath, a couple of future stars, wicketkeeper-batsman Romesh Kaluwitharana and Chandika Hathurusingha, were also a part of the Sri Lankan team. Even though Sri Lanka did not fare well in the tournament, Sanath formed friendships across teams, as it was his first official visit as a member of any representative national side.

Sanath was now a known name in Sri Lanka, but he still needed to ply his trade in Colombo to be noticed for higher honours. At that time, he was playing for Colombo Cricket Club, before moving to Bloomfield Athletic and Cricket Club. He would travel for four hours by bus one way and return home by midnight.

Eventually, Sanath decided to move to Colombo and his mother, Breeda, would often travel 118 kilometres to help him with money. 'He used to tell me to avoid these trips but I wanted to see him and also check if he needed some money,' Breeda told Mid-Day.[5]

Sanath finally got a job after the Under-19 World Cup with the Nawaloka Group, thanks to his coach Lionel Wagasinghe. The company manufactured corrugated cartons and Sanath worked there for two years. Later, after he became the national captain, he even worked as the public relations manager for NDB Bank. But it was the initial years of struggle in Colombo that shaped Sanath's career. He was one of the outstation players who lived for

---

[5]Sanjjeev K. Samyal, 'Behind Every Successful Man…', http://archive.mid-day.com/news/2008/jul/300708sports23.htm, 30 July 2008.

months in the Arjuna Ranatunga family household in Colombo's Maradana area.

'One of the first things I remember about that is that I had to switch rooms because Sanath snored too loudly,' Ranatunga spoke about the struggle during an interview to a TV show called *Inside Sports TV*. 'We didn't have everything the modern cricketers have, but my parents made sure we had enough dhal, sambol, bread and rice for the lot of us. Those kinds of things built camaraderie. We were all united. You can't get that from living and eating at hotels.'[6]

Then, Sanath moved into the home of his neighbour from Matara, Mr Dafter. In an interview to ESPNcricinfo, Sanath explained the impact of this association. 'From 1989 to 1997, he allowed me to stay in a spare room in his house (in Colombo). Mr Dafter and his wife were like my foster parents. The other was his friend Lalit Wanagasinghe. Those guys always pushed me and believed I would one day play for Sri Lanka. Coming from a small town to a big city like Colombo, one could easily lose one's way, but these two took good care of me and always gave me good advice. They would come and watch me play, and discuss cricket at the house later in the night.'[7]

What kept Sanath going in these long years of struggle were his strong Buddhist beliefs. Breeda actually believed that Sanath's success in the future was because of his good deeds in his previous life. 'Every time he is here (Matara), he goes to a famous temple

---

[6]Andrew Fidel Fernando, 'The Lion's Fairy Tale', http://www.thecricketmonthly.com/story/834255/the-lion-s-fairy-tale, March 2015.
[7]Interview by Nagraj Gollapudi, 'Winning for Sri Lanka is What I Enjoy the Most', http://www.espncricinfo.com/magazine/content/story/441226.html, 26 December 2009.

here and they tie a white thread around his wrists and that's the reason for his strength,' recalled Breeda.[8]

For Sanath, religion offered him peace. 'Each time I pray, I just ask for happiness, and to become a mentally stronger person. In recent years I have started meditating a lot and that helps me keep cool when I make my decisions.'[9]

The Sudden Limelight

Perhaps the beliefs did work wonders as Sanath quickly climbed the ladder of success. He was named a part of the high-profile Sri Lanka B, which toured Pakistan in March 1989. This was before the now prevalent A team concept became common.

The tour was meant to provide fringe cricketers of Sri Lanka some exposure before they were picked for the national side. Indeed, it proved to be the turning point in Sanath's career. Sri Lanka B was to play three unofficial Tests against a Pakistan B side, apart from five warm-up fixtures.

Sri Lanka's side featured future players like Champaka Ramanayake, Ruwan Kalpage, the Ranatunga brothers (Dhammika and Sanjeeva) and Chandika Hathurasingha. Pakistan fielded a number of their current and future stars too. Saeed Anwar, Mushtaq Ahmed and Inzamam-ul-Haq were some of the prominent names to play in that series. Apart from them, other future and current

---

[8]Sanjjeev K. Samyal, 'Behind Every Successful Man...', http://archive.mid-day.com/news/2008/jul/300708sports23.htm, 30 July 2008.
[9]Interview by Nagraj Gollapudi, 'I'd Like to Play for Another Six Months', http://www.espn.in/cricket/story/_/id/22740344/play-another-six-months, 27 December 2009.

internationals including Nadeem Ghauri, Iqbal Sikander, Wasim Haider, Iqbal Qasim, Shahid Mahboob, Mansoor Rana and Akram Raza also played in that series.

Sanath struck two successive double centuries on that tour. The first was an unbeaten 203 off 244 balls with 27 boundaries and a six at Lahore's Gaddafi Stadium. Pakistan B did not know what hit them on a hot March day in Lahore. They packed the offside field with seven fielders, but Sanath still found his gap. The second was a similar effort and he ended with an undefeated knock of 207 in 311 balls with 34 boundaries at the National Stadium in Karachi.

On tours, players usually leave their kits in the dressing room at the stadium. But Sanath tried to do something different on that tour. Deeply superstitious, Sanath would carry his bat every day after the day's play to his hotel room. And it worked wonderfully for him!

For Pakistan B, one of the successes in the series was international cricketer Mansoor Rana. He scored two centuries in the series, before he was picked for the Pakistan senior side for a series against Sri Lanka. Rana was at the receiving end of Sanath's fury in Lahore. 'Those were the days without video analysis. We used to depend on working out players only after we had played them once or twice at the A or B level. Sanath gave clear indication early on how fit he was. There was just no sign of tiredness. It was hot in Lahore at the time, but Sanath stayed strong,' recalled Mansoor Rana to the author.

Another player who faced Sanath's fury during the series was leg-spinner Mushtaq Ahmed. Both players had formed a strong bond since the inaugural Under-19 World Cup days. Sri Lanka's batsmen carried the reputation of being attractive stroke-makers, but the way Sanath dealt with Mushtaq and the others changed their perception about him forever.

'He was very quick with his hand-eye coordination even in those days (March 1989). We had Saeed Anwar in our side, but he was a more correct player. Sanath, on the other hand, even then would punish good balls by cutting you mercilessly,' Mushtaq recalled to the author.

During the course of the trip, the sides made a number of bus trips. Sanath would sit in the last row alongside medium-fast bowler Champaka Ramanayake and the two would sing all through the long journeys. Music was one of Sanath's passions and he demonstrated his skill for the first time on that Pakistan trip.

News of Sanath's double centuries also reached the senior Sri Lankan team, then on tour in Sharjah, incidentally for a series against Pakistan's senior side. Part of this trip was former Captain Duleep Mendis who was in the final leg of his international career. With Mendis on the verge of ending his career, places were about to open up in the national side. Sanath's exploits as a schoolboy cricketer and as a junior cricketer for Sri Lanka meant that he was one of the most talked-about cricketers in the country at the time.

And it Begins

Sri Lanka was to undertake a tour to Australia for a Test series and a triangular competition called World Series Cup (WSC), also involving Pakistan. Sanath was in Dafter's house when he heard about his selection for the Australia tour. The meeting had started at eight in the morning and Sanath was restlessly waiting for the outcome. Finally, he got a call from the then secretary of the Board of Control for Cricket in Sri Lanka (BCCSL) to inform him that he had been picked. The selectors had decided to gamble on Sanath as they had picked just one wicketkeeper for the tour in Hashan Tillakaratne.

By now, Arjuna Ranatunga was the leader of the side in the truest sense. Those were the days when the players in the international cricket teams would share rooms. Only the captain and the manager had the privilege of having a room to themselves. Ranatunga decided to club the younger players with the senior pros. As a result, Sanath was bunched with fast bowler Graeme Labrooy.

One of the tasks assigned to Labrooy was to groom Sanath regarding all the dos and don'ts for an international cricketer. Labrooy spent time explaining the various processes to him, which ranged from how to make tea to how to walk on the field. Another future captain, Roshan Mahanama, who would become Sanath's close friend later, was also a sounding board for Sanath throughout the tour. Labrooy and Sanath played together in Colombo for the Colombo Cricket Club (CCC). Mahanama was the other cricketer who was part of the same club and over the years, a strong bond developed between the trio.

One of the first things Labrooy did was to test Sanath with a task on the very first day of staying together. Before going to sleep, he told Sanath that he needed to make tea for both of them the next morning as part of a touring convention. Sanath promptly got up early and started fiddling with the kettle. He had never used a kettle before in his life. After seeing him struggle for a while, Labrooy decided to help him out. 'It was meant to be an easy initiation to the big stage for him,' Labrooy recalled to the author.

He was, however, being assigned tasks he had never done before. Then, the teams did not have the luxury of laundry allowance and most players on tours spent a lot of time in laundromats and ironing their clothes. The Sri Lankan team was no different in 1989–90. Sanath was surprised when he was told that he had to wash his clothes and then iron them himself. The side had a rule of fining players who did not have ironed clothes. But Sanath had never used an iron and leaned on Labrooy for help. Labrooy, as the chairman of the fine committee, had to find a balance between letting off his roommate and still appearing fair. Labrooy finally decided to help him out by ironing his clothes and taught him how to do it as well.

Even though Sanath was an inexperienced tourist, when it came to matters on the field, he seemed confident. Nothing would distract him and he adjusted well to the side, which was full of big names.

'His selection had been bit of a surprise as few of the seniors had been left out. The selectors were trying to bring in a few younger players for the experience,' said Labrooy to the author. 'But we did not see any nerves. He gelled well with the side, was very focused.'

Sanath spent a lot of time observing his seniors, assisting them even before they could ask for help. He fitted in very well.

'He went with the flow, which was significant for a boy coming from Matara. He would get up early if we had made plans to go out for a meal early. This, even after we may have slept late. Whether it was wanting to go shopping, spending time away from cricket—he was always a willing participant. He was happy to do what the majority wanted to do,' Labrooy told the author about Sanath's first tour.

In the very first week of that tour to Australia, Sanath played two state sides—New South Wales and Victoria—in two four-day games as part of the build-up to the tour. He faced

On his final tour to India in 2009–10, Sanath Jayasuriya played a small part for Sri Lanka in the Twenty20 International series with an all-round effort at Nagpur.
Photo courtesy: Narender Kumar

Sanath's golden arm always worked against India and he was in top form even on his last tour to India in 2009–10.
Photo courtesy: Narender Kumar

Sanath Jayasuriya, checking his most trusted ally on a cricket field while preparing to take on his old foe, India.
Photo courtesy: Narender Kumar

Back in the saddle: Sanath Jayasuriya returned to his role as chairman of selectors and was back in discussions with Sri Lankan head coach, Graham Ford, in 2016 during the series against Australia at R. Premadasa International Cricket Stadium in Colombo.
Photo courtesy: Lakruwan Wanniarachchi

Sri Lanka's chairman of selectors, Sanath Jayasuriya, addresses a press conference in Colombo on 7 July 2016.
Photo courtesy: Lakruwan Wanniarachchi

Sanath Jayasuriya in conversation with Sri Lankan captain, Dinesh Chandimal, at Pallekele in 2017. Photo courtesy: Lakruwan Wanniarachchi

Always ready to oblige fans and friends. Photo courtesy: Kapil Pathare

*With the man who shaped Sanath's
career, Arjuna Ranatunga.
Photo courtesy: Sanath Jayasuriya*

*Another former compatriot and
teammate, Asanka Gurusinha.
Photo courtesy: Sanath Jayasuriya*

Long-term teammates, Romesh Kaluwitharana, Upul Chandana and Roshan Mahanama.
Photo courtesy: Sanath Jayasuriya

Members of the 1996 World Cup champion squad getting together after a long time.
Photo courtesy: Sanath Jayasuriya

Sanath with an old foe and long-time friend, former Indian captain, Mohammed Azharuddin.
Photo courtesy: Sanath Jayasuriya

With fellow champion batsman, Aravinda de Silva.
Photo courtesy: Sanath Jayasuriya

With his father, Dunstan, mother, Breeda, and uncle, Rajapaksa.
Photo courtesy: Sanath Jayasuriya

With Mumbai Indians owners, Mukesh and Nita Ambani.
Photo courtesy: Sanath Jayasuriya

champions like Mark Taylor, Steve Waugh and Mark Waugh in the game against New South Wales. A week later, he played an equally adept Victorian side with internationals like Simon O'Donnell, Damien Fleming and Paul Reiffel.

Little did he know that in the match against Victoria, he had a spectator who was keenly watching him make a swift 31 off 38 balls. That man, Dav Whatmore, had been dropped by Victoria selectors, but had still made it to the Sale Oval in Sale. The knock left an impression on Whatmore, which later formed the cornerstone of a close relationship, redefining Sri Lankan cricket forever.

It was more than a month on tour in Australia before Sanath finally got the opportunity to realize his dream of playing international cricket for Sri Lanka. Before he was to make his debut in ODI cricket, he got ready advice from Labrooy—his roommate. 'It is a great opportunity. Remember very few get it. Make the most of it by sticking to your basics. Pick whatever you can from the seniors. Don't throw it away,' said Labrooy to Sanath. It was later recalled to the author. An attentive listener, Sanath did not have any questions and slept peacefully before he made his debut on what was the Boxing Day—an important landmark.

The Boxing Day, a day after Christmas, encounters a Test match in Melbourne at their iconic Melbourne Cricket Ground (MCG). It has become part of the Australian cricket culture, and this is usually followed by a Test in the New Year at the Sydney Cricket Ground (SCG).

In 1989, the Australian Cricket Board (ACB) decided to forgo that tradition. Instead, their annual World Series Cup (WSC) competition, featuring Sri Lanka and Pakistan alongside

Australia, was to begin that day. MCG was packed with more than 45,000 people.

When the debut match finally began, Sri Lanka fielded first as Captain Arjuna Ranatunga felt they could chase well. Chasing 229 for a win in the first match of the competition, Sanath walked in at number five to bat against the world champion, Australia, for the first time ever.

When he took guard, he felt something strange. He was taking guard to one of the most gregarious characters to have played the game—Mervyn Gregory Hughes. Now, Hughes was quite unlike any other fast bowler. He was 6'4", and he always sported a handlebar moustache, a belly towards the later stages of his career and a menacing look. He had been nicknamed 'Fruitfly' by his teammates because he liked to have run-ins with his rivals in what could be mildly termed as colourful language. For someone like Sanath, who was just twenty, Hughes was his first brush with what international cricket was to offer in the future. When he faced Hughes, he just could not concentrate.

'When Merv Hughes was bowling, I struggled to watch the ball,' Sanath said in his later years. 'I kept looking at his face, because it was so different. I found it really hard to come from school and club cricket, but that was the gap we had to bridge. It made us tough and I think my upbringing away from Colombo helped to make me tough as well.'[10]

No wonder Sanath did not last long and made just 3 runs in his first appearance for Sri Lanka in an international match. He was incidentally out, and the ball was caught by Greg Campbell,

---

[10]Richard Hobson, 'The Apologetic Assassin', http://www.espncricinfo.com/wisdencricketer/content/story/321846.html, December 2007.

the maternal uncle of his future rival, Ricky Ponting, off Hughes's bowling. His next tour was to Sharjah for the Australasia Cup, involving four Asian sides and two sides from the Australian continent (Australia and New Zealand).

Incidentally, his mother, Breeda, had made a wish, which he wanted to fulfil but did not know how to. She had wanted him to buy a refrigerator in Dubai and bring it back with him. He sheepishly went to Labrooy and asked him, 'My mom thinks I should bring a fridge from here.' Labrooy and Sanath then went looking for a fridge in Dubai. They finally bought one and took it back with them to Colombo. 'I remember arranging a pick-up truck once we landed in Colombo as we drove down to Matara (Sanath's hometown),' recalled Labrooy to the author.

Testing His Skill

In 1990–91, Sanath again shared a room with Labrooy during a tour to New Zealand. This was the tour in which Sanath finally made his Test debut. It was not a memorable debut, but he held his own, making a compact 35.

What also stood out in his debut at Hamilton's Seddon Park was his fielding—something he would excel at in his later years. As is the case with a debutant, Sanath was posted at the most precarious position on the field—forward short-leg. This is a position that is quite close on the leg-side right next to the batsman and almost always has the fielders in harm's way.

New Zealand sent in their fast bowler and renowned collector of ducks, Danny Morrison, as a nightwatchman in the second innings at the number-three position. Morrison was quite often the butt of all jokes for his lack of prowess with the bat. On that day, he walked out to bat, wearing the helmet of his captain, Martin Crowe, which had no grill. Morrison appeared confident.

In the fourteenth ball he faced, Morrison flicked Sri Lanka's medium-fast bowler Champaka Ramanayake off his legs. Sanath crouched in his position, with the ball stuck in his armpit. From there it moved to his elbow, before finally resting on his bicep. It was a freak catch made possible only because Sanath had stayed down. The forward short-leg position was never Sanath's natural fielding area, so it made the catch even more commendable. He leapt with joy as he celebrated his first catch in Test cricket. 'I still cannot forget that moment. He (Sanath) got in my way of getting a big score,' joked Morrison about that freak dismissal.

On that tour to New Zealand, Sanath caught the eye of former West Indies captain Alvin Kallicharan with his fielding. Kalli, as he is known, was in New Zealand at the time and was drafted in to work with the Sri Lankan side. Kalli was very impressed with his ability to cover a field swiftly. He likened him to the popular Warner Brothers animated cartoon character Speedy Gonzales, who could run extremely fast. This was perhaps a result of playing on the beach of Matara in his early years.

During the course of the series, Sanath also caught Kalli's attention with his brisk knocks. 'He came looking for Sanath after one of the matches. He had a lot of time for him. He was holding his forearms and really liked what he saw. The strength in them (forearms) was what made him sit up and take notice,' Ramanayake recalled to the author.

What followed next was a tour to England for a one-off Test, as was the norm for Sri Lanka at that stage. But the tour also featured a number of warm-up fixtures against some of the best county sides. Sanath played well in most of the matches. He was particularly impressive in the match against Worcestershire and then in the one against Somerset. He then carried his form into the one-off Test with a typically aggressive 66—his first Test half-century—in only his third Test. It seemed like Sanath was finally coming into his own.

But it was not until December of 1991 that Sanath emerged out of the shadows of his most illustrious seniors like Aravinda de Silva and Ranatunga, among others. Sanath exceeded all expectations on the tour as he logged 238 runs from the three Test series to emerge as the highest run-getter on either side. Considering that the Pakistan side at the time featured the likes of Javed Miandad and Imran Khan, alongside the deadly pace bowling duo of Wasim Akram and Waqar Younis, Sanath's achievement made everyone sit up and take notice.

It so happened that the two left-handers, Sanath and Tillakaratne, were the only ones who were able to handle the fury of the reverse swing of Pakistan's pace battery. This was also the last time Imran played in Test matches but the series slowly faded from everyone's memories as it was played just a month before the 1992 Cricket World Cup.

Knocking on the World Stage

When the World Cup got underway, Sanath featured in only six of the nine league games that Sri Lanka played. Sri Lanka won just two games in the tournament, beating both African nations—newcomer South Africa and Zimbabwe—by an identical three-wicket margin. Sanath had a part to play in both the wins.

In the win against Zimbabwe, which resulted in the highest-ever chase in an ODI at the time, Sanath contributed a swift 32 off 24 balls. Sri Lanka chased down Zimbabwe's 312 for 4 with 4 balls and 3 wickets to spare at New Plymouth. Ranatunga was the cornerstone of the victory with an unbeaten 88.

Against South Africa, Sanath showed his versatility on the field as he plucked out two amazing catches. The first one was during Ranatunga's bowling as he leapt high to pluck a catch off Mark Rushmere. 'If that is not part of the classic catches contest, then I am a Dutchman,' commented veteran English broadcaster Henry Blofield on air at the time.

In the next one—this time at extra cover—Sanath again leapt and snatched to dismiss Jonty Rhodes off Pramodya Wickaramasinghe at a very windy Wellington. Even for Jonty who was to set new standards with his fielding at the time, this came as a shock. Those two catches by Sanath turned the tide for Sri Lanka as they registered a hard-fought win. Despite such feats, the World Cup was a forgettable exercise for Sri Lanka and there was no indication then of the heights they would reach four years later.

Regular attacks by the Liberation Tigers of Tamil Eelam (LTTE) in the country meant that international cricket was drying up. Australia toured Sri Lanka in 1992, but doubts about the situation in the country remained. The matter came to a head when New Zealand toured in December 1992. The Kiwi team was in town when an attack took place in Colombo and a second string side of New Zealand replaced the players on tour. International cricket in Sri Lanka then took a massive beating because of the security situation. Sanath was still not a regular in the side, and his appearances in both formats were quite irregular.

In January of 1993, he was named the captain of a Sri Lanka Under-24 side to tour South Africa. This was to be the first official tour by a representative Sri Lankan side to South Africa since its return to the global cricket fold in 1991. Sanath was to lead a side that included future stars like Marvan Atapattu, Romesh Kaluwitharana and Muttiah Muralitharan. Additionally, there were other players who had either featured in international cricket or were on the verge of breaking in like Ruwan Kalpage and Pramodya Wickramasinghe.

On the tour, Sri Lanka played just one unofficial Test against South Africa Under-24, but faced off against the provincial sides in warm-up fixtures. However, what is still talked about is Sanath's knock off 126 against a Natal Under-24 side in Durban. That Natal side included, among others, Shaun Pollock, who was to captain South African national side in the future. It also included prospective South African all-rounders like Dale Benkenstein and Derek Crookes, apart from Zimbabwe's Neil Johnson.

Watching Sanath play closely at the historic Wanderers was South Africa's former all-rounder and national coach at the time, Mike Procter, at the time—and he was mighty impressed with what he saw. 'I still remember that innings very well, because I have not seen anything better than that. It is the ease with which he scored that stands out in mind. It was a combination of a quality player taking on a good attack which gives you a real joy,' Procter said to the author.

Seated alongside Procter and watching Sanath bat was a champion of his craft, former West Indies fast bowler, the late Malcolm Marshall. Out of the West Indies side, Marshall was then plying his trade for Natal's senior side. Marshall, too, was impressed with what he saw.

In the unofficial Test that followed, Sri Lanka took on South Africa, which was led by future disgraced captain, the late Hansie Cronje. Also playing for the South African side were Jonty Rhodes and fast bowler Brett Schultz. Though he failed in both the innings, Sanath's intent stuck in the minds of the South Africans who played the match. South Africa was to tour Sri Lanka later in 1993, so the knowledge about Sanath came handy.

Coming into Focus

When Sanath returned home, it was time to play against bamboozled Englishmen already at sixes and sevens, thanks to Indian spinners led by Anil Kumble. Little did the Englishmen know that there were more trials by spin in store when it came to Sri Lanka as well. This resulted in England's first-ever Test match loss to Sri Lanka. As if to round off the disappointment, Sanath spun a web around England at Moratuwa in the final ODI of the tour. Sanath ended with a 6 for 29—the best at the time for Sri Lanka in ODI cricket. On the other hand, a harrowed English side had had enough of the spin diet and looked for excuses to sum up a forgettable winter.

The English press also played its part in looking for reasons for Sanath picking six wickets. *The Independent*'s Glenn Moore described the spell of Sanath thus: 'Several batsmen were out heaving across the line to a series of bowlers who would only be seen in the County Championship when a declaration was being set up. Sanath Jayasuriya, who turns the ball but rarely pitches it correctly, took a mind-boggling 5 for 14 in his last 21 balls as he ended with 6 for 29.'[11]

But teammate Ramanayake completely disagreed with the

---

[11]Glenn Moore, 'Cricket: England Leave in More Shame', *Independent*, https://www.independent.co.uk/sport/cricket-england-leave-in-more-shame-1498948.html, 21 March 1993.

assessment. 'He was turning quite a bit that day. He showed why he did the magic turn with the ball always. He was a man with the golden arm.'

Sanath's effort with the ball that day in Moratuwa made sure to secure a mention in all future quizzes on cricket when it came to guessing who held the record for the best bowling figures for Sri Lanka. It took special efforts from Muralitharan and Chaminda Vaas to displace Sanath as the answer to that question in the future.

Sanath was now slowly moving ahead to gain a regular place in the shorter format, but in Tests, the selectors still used him intermittently. It required a brisk 65 against the touring South African side in September 1993 to strengthen his claim. 'He counter-attacked very well and showed that he was not going to hold back. He came in at number seven and really stood out with his approach,' Schultz recalled to the author. Even though Sanath continued to prosper with the bat in the ODI format in Sharjah in October 1993, he was still not consistent enough.

Cast in a New Role

In November 1993, India hosted its first ODI tournament—a five-nation CAB Jubilee tournament—in coloured clothing with white balls and black sight screens. Sri Lanka also attempted something new in the tournament when they pushed Sanath into opening the innings for the first time.

This experiment of Sri Lanka took place in a cricketing outpost in Patna. In the league match against Zimbabwe at the Moin-ul-Haq Stadium, Sri Lanka pushed Sanath into opening the batting with Mahanama. He continued to open for the rest of the tournament. Though he did not prove to be an instant success, a seed for his future triumph had been planted.

Meanwhile, internal strife cropped up in the side, when Ranatunga stood up for his deputy Aravinda de Silva. Former Test captain and then Sri Lanka Coach Bandula Warnapura had laid down fitness as paramount for selection. De Silva failed this test and was dropped for the April 1994 Australasia Cup in Sharjah. In protest, Ranatunga boycotted the tournament.

As a result, Mahanama led almost a second string side to Sharjah. It was not a great time for Sri Lankan cricket as it looked like it had been split right in the middle. Sanath was too junior a player at the time to get involved. Player power finally won and the senior professionals were restored to the side while Coach Warnapura was sacked. This was when the best phase of Sanath's ODI career began. He started off with three successive half-centuries against Pakistan in August 1994.

Sanath was to then announce his arrival as an ODI opener in a big way. He smashed 140 off 143 balls (9 boundaries and 6 sixes) against New Zealand at Bloemfontein, South Africa, in the four-nation Mandela Trophy in December 1994. At that time, this was the highest individual ODI score by a Sri Lankan.

The only New Zealand bowler to challenge him during his knock was medium-fast bowler Chris Pringle. Proving that he had learnt from his struggles against Pringle, Sanath came back with a vengeance in the return game against New Zealand.

He followed up with a 31-ball 52 with 5 boundaries and 3 sixes in East London. This time, Sanath was particularly severe on Pringle. He dealt with Pringle with utter disdain and this knock has stayed fresh in the memory of the New Zealand bowler. 'You could see that here was a batsman who was learning very quickly. He was the first player I saw getting better with every game,' Pringle said to the author, about the knock. In many ways, Pringle felt Sanath reminded him of his own teammate Nathan Astle who was as destructive, but started off first as a middle-order batsman before moving on to the opener's role. Sanath was to better this performance many times in the future, but the world was now looking at him in a different way. The tide was about to turn for Sri Lankan cricket forever in the new year of 1995 and Sanath would continue to rise in stature.

2

Opening in Style

In December of 1995, astronomers at the NASA announced that they had found a planet, 51 Pegassi B, outside our solar system. Earlier that year, the *James Bond* movies made a return to the big screen after six years. For the world at large, there was plenty to look forward to that year.

In the smaller ecosystem of cricket, the good news was the coming of age of Sri Lanka as a cricketing nation. Until then, Sri Lanka had been a side that could cause a surprise or two, take a game off a side in a tour, but could never challenge anyone. But that year in 1995, everything changed.

First, in February–March 1995, Sri Lanka registered their first-ever Test series victory away from home when they won in New Zealand by 1-0. The side gained a lot of confidence from the win. The problems of the previous few years when captain Arjuna Ranatunga had faced troubles and disciplinary action had finally disappeared. The side appeared to have gained experience as a core group of players stuck together.

Things really started to change for Sri Lanka when they toured Pakistan for a full series. By now, the BCCSL had recruited a full-time professional team coach. This man was Dav Whatmore, a former Sri Lankan-Australian Test cricketer who was then a coach at the Victoria Institute of Sport in Melbourne. This move by BCCSL is still considered as the turning point in the history of Sri Lankan cricket. From here on, Sri Lankan started a new journey and Whatmore played a key role in the transformation.

'Dav wasn't one to tinker with techniques, but he brought two very important things to Sri Lankan cricket: method and systems,' said Sidath Wettimuny, Sri Lanka's selector at the time, in 1995–96, to ESPNcricinfo. 'We were players in the '60s, '70s and '80s, who were part-time, fun cricketers. Dav had a big drive to get us training and thinking like professionals.'[12]

Sri Lanka had always been ahead of the curve in the subcontinent in terms of professional appointments, having used the services of greats like Sir Garfield Sobers and Alvin Kallicharan as coaches in the past. Whatmore brought in a qualified physiotherapist, Australian Alex Kontouris, as well to provide the side verve and direction.

'Sri Lanka became a professional unit only after Whatmore came. Alex Kontouris, the physio, was another man who brought in a big and immediate change, because he put in place a system

---

[12]Andrew Fidel Fernando, 'The Lion's Fairy Tale', http://www.thecricketmonthly.com/story/834255/the-lion-s-fairy-tale, March 2015.

for training and physical fitness,' Sanath recalled their contribution years later.[13]

The duo made an instant impact as Sri Lanka won a Test series in Pakistan for the first time, by 2–1, after having lost the first Test. They also won the ODI series by 2–1. That was followed by a title triumph in Sharjah when Sri Lanka won a tri-nation tournament for the first time after beating West Indies and Pakistan.

'Those two tours (Pakistan and Sharjah) were really the turning points. We did extremely well on those two tours and that gave a lot of confidence to the sides,' said Duleep Mendis, then captain and team manager, to the author.

Throughout this period of success, Sanath was still a minor player in the bigger scheme of things. He was not part of the Tests in either New Zealand or Pakistan and had a minor role as the opener in the ODIs. He had still not set the world on fire. In fact, there had also been a call to select Sanath for the Tests in Pakistan, but the team management had opted against it.

So, we are still about six months away from Sanath arriving on the big stage.

On Top, Down Under

Sri Lanka was to tour Australia for their first full series featuring a three-Test series and a tri-series also involving West Indies as the third team. This tour changed everything, not just for Sri Lankan cricket, but also for Sanath.

[13]Interview by Nagraj Gollapudi, 'Winning for Sri Lanka is What I Enjoy the Most', http://www.espncricinfo.com/magazine/content/story/441226. html, 26 December 2009.

There were problems galore right through the Test matches, especially when the then young spinner Muttiah Muralitharan was repeatedly called by umpire Darrell Hair for what he perceived to be an illegal action. An angry Ranatunga took it upon himself to fight for his side. This really united the side.

Meanwhile, Sanath, still not a prominent player, continued to be away from the Test matches, but blazed at times during the ODIs. This caught Coach Whatmore's attention.

'He was a very good fielder. He bowled as well and opened the batting. He thrashed the ball through the off-side. He was a very good package to have in the shorter format, easy to say, good package in that format,' said Whatmore of his first impressions of Sanath.

But he was still to become the force he would be in 1996. His highest score in the ODI tri-series was just 30. Sri Lanka, too, had started off with a couple of losses in the tri-series. Roshan Mahanama had been Sri Lanka's opening batsman for long and Sanath had collaborated with Mahanama with limited success— but that was not enough. It was then that something clicked in the mind of the manager, Mendis.

'There was a time then that Kalu was batting well but he was not keeping well. I just had an idea, why not open with Kalu so as to give free hand to Sanath as well,' Mendis told Ranatunga and Whatmore. It was later recalled to the author.

That suggestion hit Whatmore hard. 'It was like light coming into a dark room. Kalu was a sweet timer of the ball. He was getting caught in the deep playing shots, not slogging. I thought to myself, "S**t man, let's do it,"' said Whatmore to the author.

Though the partnership did not set Australia on fire, the very idea of two batsmen striking in the first 15 overs of an ODI was appealing. In those days, an ODI used to have field restrictions where just two fielders were outside a 30-yard circle. India's Krishnamachari Srikkanth was a pioneer of the exploitation of this rule in the 1980s. Then, in the 1992 World Cup, England used Sir Ian Botham and New Zealand employed Mark Greatbatch to make the most of the rule.

But midway, it seemed like teams forgot to make the most of the rule. This is why the sudden appearance of Sanath and Kaluwitharana hit everyone hard. There was no instruction from the team to strike at a particular rate out of fear that it might put pressure on them. The duo was just told to play their natural game and Sanath managed to feed off Kaluwitharana's approach.

'When he (Kaluwitharana) got going, he made things easier for me at the other end. He could hit the ball very hard, played all the shots. He was really talented and made batting look easy. He was as confident as me. I remember he failed for 20 innings once, but Arjuna gave him the chance, knowing he was a match-winner,' Sanath explained later.[14]

While Kaluwitharana scored three half-centuries, Sanath was yet to find his true form. But that was when bad luck struck. Mahanama, troubled by the knock on the knuckles of his left hand, was pulled out of the third Test at Adelaide. It was then out of compulsion, that Sanath was pushed up the order to open in a Test match. This would be the first time he would open in the longer format.

'We were changing the order constantly because of injuries.

---

[14]Interview by Nagraj Gollapudi, 'Winning for Sri Lanka is What I Enjoy the Most', http://www.espncricinfo.com/magazine/content/story/441226. html, 26 December 2009.

Some things worked, some did not. We decided to throw him a challenge,' said Mendis to the author. Sanath accepted it happily, as he could score off his back foot on the true-natured pitches of Australia.

Sanath scored 48 in the first innings and then followed it up with a stroke-filled 112 (188 balls: 14 boundaries and 2 sixes). This was his first Test century leading to wild celebration from the lone Sri Lankan fan running around with a flag at the Adelaide Oval. He received a standing ovation from all.

'I was really happy to get a century against such a good bowling attack, which included Shane Warne. It was scored under pressure against one of the best Test teams in the world. When you do that, you get a nice feeling in your system,' said Sanath[15] about the knock, which he believed changed his career forever.

The tour may not have ended favourably for the Sri Lankan side, but it bonded them as a unit. They were first accused of ball tampering, and then the umpiring left them harrowed. They were also accused of possessing oversized logos and then there was the whole fracas around Murali's action. With the feeling of being cornered by everyone in Australia, the Sri Lankan cricketers left the shores feeling a lot more motivated. With the World Cup 1996 just around the corner, this was just the tonic they needed to perform better.

Cup of Dreams

There was a lot of speculation over whether Sri Lanka would be able to host matches owing to persistent threats from the LTTE. Just 18 days before the World Cup, there was a vicious attack,

---

[15]Ibid.

which left 91 dead and injured as many as 1,400. Even the most persistent assurances could not convince the Australian and West Indies sides to travel to Sri Lanka to play their league matches in Colombo. Both sides pulled out and forfeited the contest.

As a result, Sri Lanka got easy points from the two games, making their passage to the quarter-final a cakewalk. A joint Indo-Pak XI featuring the likes of Wasim Akram, Mohammed Azharuddin, Sachin Tendulkar, amongst others, made a dash to Colombo to play with Sri Lanka. This was to send a strong message to the other sides.

India was the first one to get a message from Sanath in New Delhi and that was the game that made Sri Lanka feel like they could get deep into the tournament. Sri Lanka made mincemeat of India's total of 271 as Sanath and Kaluwitharana wreaked havoc on a gloomy day in the Indian capital.

'In the team meetings we never really spoke about run rate in the first 15 overs. We could be wickets down for no runs, but it did not matter as we had five more batsmen who could get hundreds. That India game changed my mind because it showed two sides with a contrasting approach. It made us believe that we could be competitive against anyone,' Whatmore said to the author.

Against Kenya, Sanath and Kaluwitharana raised 83 off 40 balls to set the tone for Aravinda de Silva's assault, paving the way for an easy win and an easy passage through to the quarter-final. The Sri Lankan team finally felt like it was getting somewhere. It was then time to fly to Faisalabad in Pakistan to take on England in the quarter-final.

On this flight, Sanath was seated next to former Sri Lankan cricketer Sidath Wettimuny, who was then a selector and a manager with PILCOM (Pakistan India Lanka Organising Committee). In one of the chats about life with Wettimuny, Sanath mentioned something that stayed with him. 'I need another (Sri Lankan) ₹175,000 to get the roof built in my house. If that happens, nothing else matters for me,' Sanath told Wettimuny, exhibiting his simple thinking.

On the rest of the journey, there was a time when Sanath was reading the in-flight magazine and spotted a luxury watch. He instantly turned to Wettimuny and joked, 'If I get a 50 (against England), will you buy me this watch?' Wettimuny offered him a challenge instead. 'You bat 15 overs and the watch is yours. That's my promise.'

The travel day was not great as it felt compressed for both sides. England opted to not practise, but Sri Lanka felt the need to have a light session. The session lasted for about 30 minutes, with each member getting 10 minutes. The purpose of the exercise was to show commitment and make the effort.

With that challenge in mind, Sanath set about finishing off England in the quarter-final. England made a modest 235 for 8 wickets, and in response, Sanath destroyed them. He raced to 82 off just 44 balls.

Sanath teed off and finished yet another career, this time that of left-armed Richard Illingworth. He then reduced Phil Defreitas to bowling off-spin, much like what he had done with Manoj Prabhakar when he was playing against India.

By the time he got out in the twelfth over, Sanath had set a rollicking pace for the chase to be completed without any pressure. The moment he entered the dressing room at the Iqbal Stadium, he sought out Wettimuny to remind him of his promise.

'Have I won the watch?' he asked Wettimuny. But the former Sri Lankan cricketer flatly refused because Sanath had not honoured his half of the bargain. 'Remember the bet was for 15 overs. You were out in 12 overs.' Eventually, after a day, Wettimuny did honour his promise and gifted him the watch.

Post the easy Sri Lankan win with 9 overs and 5 wickets to spare, the English all-rounder Dermot Reeve stood outside the Sri Lankan team's dressing room and hollered. 'Sanath, you've ruined my career,' he said. 'But I'm going to go home and put £600 on you guys, so you had better win.'[16] This Sri Lankan victory affected the English psyche like never before. The next morning (on 10 March 1996), the British papers had some bombastic headlines.

END OF THE WORLD FOR PATHETIC ENGLAND
Sunday Mirror

HAPLESS, HOPELESS, HUMILIATED
The Independent

WE MUST GET RID OF LORD'S LOSERS
News of the World

There were some critical comments in the English papers as well:

The England team and the system which produces it is a heavy lorry in the slow lane being passed by a succession of sports cars.

Christopher Martin-Jenkins, *Daily Telegraph*

There appears to be no spirit of adventure left in English cricket, either on or off the field.

Derek Pringle, *The Independent*

---

[16]Andrew Fidel Fernando, 'The Lion's Fairy Tale', http://www. thecricketmonthly.com/story/834255/the-lion-s-fairy-tale, March 2015.

The stage was now set for Sri Lanka to raise the bar. They travelled to Calcutta to play their co-host, India, in the semi-final. The nature of the pitch was a subject of speculation. Coach Whatmore was a worried man as he did not consider himself a good reader of the pitch. But both Mendis and Ranatunga were clear that the pitch at Eden Gardens wouldn't last, so they decided to bat first. This was going to be a change in strategy, but one they had to make considering the pitch dynamics.

The Indian team was obsessed with Sanath and they got him out, along with Kaluwitharana, but despite that, Sri Lanka managed a decent 250. With the pitch creating all sorts of problems, Whatmore felt Sanath could be a force with the ball as well.

'He comes with a round-arm action; bowls at a decent pace. His deliveries grip and make it very difficult for batsmen to negotiate. Some would spin a lot and make it difficult for a batsman to play him,' assessed Whatmore. Sanath did play his part by removing Tendulkar to seal the contest for good. The match was Sri Lanka's and so was a place in the grand finals at Lahore, against Australia.

That night in Calcutta still brings nightmares for an average Indian cricket fan. The sight of every Indian batsman being rendered clueless against Sanath and his fellow spinners is something no one has been able to get over. The situation when the entire Eden Gardens was up in arms against the feeble Indian batting has stayed in the memories of cricket fans. The reactions were so extreme that the fans threw various objects at the boundary riders. But that was hardly Sri Lanka's fault.

The sight of the gentle giant match-referee Clive Lloyd coming out to have a chat with the umpires and Ranatunga is still vivid. When the fatal final call of ending the match was taken, Sanath and the rest of the Sri Lankan fielders celebrated like never before. The thumping of the wrists as a group is a picture that tells a story, as does the sight of India's lone surviving specialist batsman Vinod Kambli walking off in tears. The journey from Calcutta to Lahore for the World Cup finals also signified a giant leap in Sri Lanka's cricket history.

Yet again, the Sri Lankan team made it a point to train under lights while the Australian team was away at an official function. This was the reason why Sri Lanka was better prepared and was aware of the dew at Gaddafi Stadium. Sanath, along with other spinners, played a part in restricting Australia. But Sanath failed this time, only to show that he is human after all. He began with typical flourish, but it did not last long as he challenged the fielding of an alert Australian side. He was beaten by Glenn McGrath's swift throw from the third man region. The veterans in the line-up, however, completed the chase quite easily.

It was a historic moment for Sri Lankan cricket as they were crowned the World Champion in ODI cricket. Sanath was named the Most Valuable Player (MVP) for the tournament. He had certainly grown in stature during the course of the tournament and he was certain to win a number of accolades for the same. The entire side was given an official reception by the Sri Lankan government after they returned home. But there was more in store for Sanath.

Sanath and the opening bowler Pramodya Wickremasinghe were given a rousing reception in Matara, organized by the Old Servatius Sport Club. The pair was taken on a motorcade to the Kotuwegoda Grounds where there was a public meeting in their honour, attended by a large crowd.

On the cricketers' request, the entire crowd maintained two minutes of silence to honour the heroes who sacrificed their entire lives playing Sri Lanka. Also present at the felicitation was skipper Ranatunga who urged people of Matara to look at Sanath and Wickremasinghe as role models.

That Sanath was emerging as the poster boy for the unconventional was further confirmed when he was chosen as one of the five Wisden cricketers for the year 1997. Sanath was the first exception of the Wisden rule of naming only cricketers who had played in England. Sanath also became the third Sri Lankan in its 134-year-old history to be part of the Wisden elite list, after Wettimuny (1985) and de Silva (1996).

Considered cricket's Bible, *Wisden Cricket Monthly* praised Sanath in a piece, paying glowing tributes to his exploits:

It is a mark of cricket's changing emphasis that Jayasuriya is celebrated not for years of consistent achievement in five-day Tests, but for a brief outpouring of intemperate stroke play in a one-day tournament in the emotive atmosphere of the subcontinent. Traditionalists may be wary of the accolade. But all those who witnessed Jayasuriya's audacious attacking batsmanship—most particularly against India, in a group match in Delhi, and England, in the quarter-final in Faisalabad—gaped in admiration.

This was combustible stroke play that challenged our assumptions. Steady starts...playing yourself in...wickets in hand...such tenets had been adapted, for sure, to the demands of one-day cricket, but never so freely abandoned. Jayasuriya's method of playing himself in seemed to consist of taking three steps down the pitch and carving the ball high over cover. He was batting as if in a baseball diamond, entirely overtaken by attacking intent. The defensive policy adopted by England's openers, Geoff Boycott and Mike Brearley, in the second World Cup final at Lord's in 1979 seemed the stuff of a different age.

However unexpected his World Cup exploits were, he is no overnight sensation. Rather more, this is the story of a man who persevered in the face of considerable hardships, and when success finally came, enthralled millions.

Sanath also became the seventh Sri Lankan to be honoured by *Indian Cricket Annual*, in its 50th year of publication. Stanley Jayasinghe (1965), Somachandra de Silva and David Heyn (1976), Duleep Mendis (1983), Ravi Ratnayeke (1987), and de Silva (1990) were the others to earn the honour before him.

The *Annual* praised him thus:

> His batting was a curious mix of science, magic and madness, based on quickness of hand and eye, and a willingness to do what is pretty dangerous—and dirty—work. That Jayasuriya won the 'Most Valuable Player' award was due to a handful of runs and wickets that were worth their weight in the World Cup for sheer timing.
>
> It is timing which is the very essence of one-day cricket—coming good on the day, at the hour, in the mere minutes which decides which way a match is going to swing. The award had an altogether different ring to it and required different credentials. For the world champions, Jayasuriya was the magic trump who turned up every time the Lankans sought something inspirational.

Making His Way to the Top

One team that Sri Lanka had not played against throughout the World Cup was Pakistan. It was speculated that one side that could challenge Sri Lanka's batting was Pakistan—with their superior bowling attack. Pakistan did not have to wait for long to be at the wrong side of Sanath's exploits. The opportunity came just two weeks after Sri Lanka became World Champion, in what can only be termed as a cricketing outpost in Singapore. The city-nation was to host a three-nation tournament, featuring India, Pakistan and Sri Lanka. This was going to be a brief tournament, lasting a week, with each side playing each other once before the final.

There were a number of subtexts in the tournament. All sides had a point to prove. Pakistan was still smarting from the loss to India in the World Cup quarter-final. India had been condemned by Sri Lanka not once but twice in the same tournament. On the other hand, the Sri Lankan team had to prove to the world that it was worthy of the title.

The tournament was to be staged in what was essentially a multisport field at the historic Singapore Cricket Club (SCC), established in 1852. The ground was bang in the centre of the city with a number of government buildings and offices surrounding the area. The venue was located between the two main streets, St. Andrew's Road and Connaught Drive, which carried heavy traffic round the clock. The ground itself was only about 65 yards, oval-shaped, with the square boundaries being not more than 58 yards away.

So even before the tournament began, Singapore Cricket Association (SCA) had to insure itself against big shot damages to cars or buses on the adjoining street. The venue itself was to undergo many makeshift arrangements, but this damage to cars by big shots was a major worry for SCA. The fine was to range from Singapore $500 to $1000 for any damages.

SCA obviously had to act with a lot of alacrity because the tournament was to feature possibly the biggest threat to the passing cars around Singapore—Sanath Jayasuriya.

The tournament started off with a rain-affected clash between Sri Lanka and Pakistan, but was replayed the next day. India arrived just 24 hours before their first match of the tournament. The Pakistan vs Sri Lanka contest was a battle between the best bowling attack and the most exciting batting line-up at the time. Even before the match began, the Pakistan bowling line-up was challenging their own teammates.

Champion fast bowler Waqar, mainstay of Pakistan attack in the absence of an injured captain Wasim Akram, challenged his fellow bowlers in chaste Punjabi, 'Kaun hai woh sher da baccha jo unho phadega (Who is the lion who has the guts to destroy Sanath)?' His fellow bowlers, especially the young off-spinner Saqlain Mushtaq who was in the first six months of his international career, was filled with trepidation. He had heard a lot about Sanath and his batting prowess. This talk worried him further about his own future in international cricket.

When Sanath walked out to bat in the replay of the first match of the tournament, the Pakistani bowlers ended up feeling as if he was indeed the only 'sher' (lion) on the field at that time. 'We had heard stories about how Sanath used to climb coconut trees and how that helped him develop strong forearms,' said Saqlain, as the legend of Sanath gained currency.

In that first match, Sanath began from where he had left off in the World Cup. He did not spare any of the Pakistani bowlers.

He even targeted the cars and the adjoining City Hall with his big hits! The SCA officials were thankful for their farsighted approach.

Saqlain was brought in early by stand-in captain Aamir Sohail to stem the flow in the first 15 overs within the restriction of overs. Saqlain chose to be conservative and hoped to restrict him by bowling a leg-side line. But his captain was not impressed. Frustrated with the lack of success, Sohail decided to bowl a left-arm spin. That turned out to be one of the biggest mistakes of his captaincy career.

After the first ball was a wide, Sanath took Sohail apart by smashing him for a boundary followed by 4 successive sixes. The ball kept sailing out of the ground, and Sohail could only smile and shrug his shoulders each time.

'When someone is batting with so much confidence, all you can do is just shrug your shoulders. That's the only thing you can do when someone is going great guns. You have to respect your opponent when he plays like that,' Sohail recalled that over.

By the end of the over, Sanath had taken 29 runs off the bat and Sohail had conceded 30 runs off that over. It turned out to be a world record for most runs conceded in an over in an ODI. It was a record that stayed until the 2007 World Cup at St. Kitts, West Indies—11 years later, when South Africa's Herschelle Gibbs struck 6 sixes off Netherlands' Dan van Bunge.

Sohail was on commentary duty at the time and was asked by a fellow commentator if he would have liked to commiserate with the bowler. 'I don't really know if I want to commiserate with the bowler. I can only say this much: I am happy that I am off the record books,' said Sohail on air at the time.

Sanath was to set two more records in the same game. He struck a record 11 sixes in the match, breaking West Indies'

Gordon Greenidge's 8 in an innings against India. He then broke the record for the fastest century when he reached the milestone off just 48 balls, bettering India's captain Mohammed Azharuddin's effort off 62 balls. Sadly, if you were not at the ground that day in Singapore, chances are you would not have seen the match anywhere else, as there was no coverage of the cricket on television in the city because of a no dish antennae-rule. Singapore had enforced a ban on satellite dishes on the premise under the pretext that unrestricted access to foreign programmes would be detrimental to national interests. Undesirable influences such as pornography were frequently cited as examples.

Saqlain's steadfast approach while bowling to Sanath finally worked as he dismissed him and he won a mini battle against his captain, Sohail. But Sri Lanka won that high-scoring contest against Pakistan quite easily. This was the time when Pakistan had the first taste of Sanath's assault. At the end of the day, the man who had challenged his fellow bowlers, Waqar, was exasperated with the experience. Over dinner with his friends, he joked with his friends, 'If this guy (Sanath) is going to bat like this, I am not coming back to a cricket field.'

Saqlain had a simpler theory to get back at Sanath. He decided to learn a couple of lines in Sinhalese to confuse Sanath. 'I learnt two lines: *'Sitlo watlo gene'* (Go have some cold water) and *'Sube udesna'* (Good morning). After that (Singapore knock) whenever I played Sanath, I used these two lines to confuse him. He would give me a mischievous smile as if to say to himself, "I have got these guys,"' recalled Saqlain.

Sanath had achieved the impossible at the time—putting Pakistan's famed bowling line-up under pressure. He did fail against

India, but there was more breathtaking batting in store in the finals against Pakistan.

On the eve of the final, Sohail hoped that he would have better luck against Sanath. 'Of course, he (Sanath) is capable of tearing apart any bowling attack on his day and I would like to see him back in the dressing room as soon as possible. I have been talking to Waqar (Younis) and Aqib (Javed) and have chalked out a plan,' said Sohail.[17]

But those plans did not work as Pakistan set about defending a modest 215. Sanath and his partner Kaluwitharana walked out to yet again set a pace that was difficult to match. It was Sanath who took off first and kept hitting mercilessly. Sanath was so quick off the blocks that Kaluwitharana hardly got a chance to take a strike. Sanath struck yet another record, reaching a half-century off just 17 balls, bettering Australia's Simon O'Donnell's 18-ball effort against Sri Lanka. All this while, Kaluwitharana had still not opened his account. Sohail was running out of ideas, but Sanath was racing away. It was so surreal that when Kaluwitharana fell with the team total on 70, he had a grand score of zero!

But thereafter, the tide turned. Sanath lost the battle of wits against Waqar. 'The pitch was getting abrasive and so reverse swing was in play. We worked out a plan where we kept feeding him outside the off-stump with a packed field and an open leg-side. He finally fell for the bait,' recalled Sohail.

That opened the floodgates as Pakistan finally showed their bowling might and closed out the contest to register an unlikely

---

[17]Samiul Hasan, 'Hard Pakistan, Lanka Battle in Singapore Final Today', http://www.espncricinfo.com/story/_/id/23273566/hard-pakistan-lanka-battle-singapore-final-today, 7 April 1996.

43-run win. This was Pakistan's first tournament win of any kind in over two years. It had seemed unlikely when Sanath was still in play, but it finally happened. That evening, as Sanath walked through the SCC, there was an acknowledgement of his exploits.

'On the final night, Jayasuriya walked through the Singapore Cricket Club bar and everyone rose to applaud him, including four ex-international captains and that is a memory that will stay with me to the end (or until I get Alzheimer's),' wrote former Australian captain Ian Chappell, then on duty as a television commentator in Singapore.[18]

For Coach Whatmore, this tournament in Singapore changed Sanath forever. 'He was a confident cricketer. But I think it was in Singapore that he transitioned from being a junior to one of the seniors in the team.'

Right after the Singapore sojourn, Sri Lanka was off to West Indies for two ODIs, followed by a trip to the United States of America (USA) for two festival games. This trip to the USA confirmed Sanath's growth as a cricketer. At a gala function to celebrate the side, most questions posed by the expat Americans and Canadians of Sri Lankans were for Sanath.

Whatmore, who was seen by many as the man behind Sri Lanka's rise, left his role in December 1996. Reports at the time suggested that Whatmore had a fallout with Ranatunga, which meant that his position became untenable. He was replaced by another former Australian cricketer—Bruce Yardley.

Meanwhile, Sanath generated a wave of prototypes from other teams in 1996. India assigned a similar role to Ajay Jadeja, but he

[18]Ian Chappell, 'Let's Hear it For the Veterans', http://www.espncricinfo.com/magazine/content/story/352238.html, 25 May 2008.

failed. England opted for a dasher in Alistair Brown in ODIs at home and that too did not succeed. Pakistan always had dashing starts from Sohail and his partner Saeed Anwar. But towards the end of 1996, Pakistan decided to step up their opening blast. At a quadrangular in Nairobi, they too gambled with a sixteen-year-old Shahid Afridi. It proved to be an immediate success as Afridi paid Sri Lanka back for the Singapore misery by smashing Sanath's record for the fastest century in 11 balls. To add insult to injury, Afridi took 28 runs off Sanath during that knock to extract a sort of revenge for his side.

Despite that setback in Nairobi, Sanath was steadily gaining reputation across the globe. He was in a lot of demand, and at the height of his popularity, he was signed up to play club cricket in Bangladesh.

Imitation is the Best Form of Flattery

Dhaka's Premier Division League is one of the most fiercely contested tournaments in the world. Some of the world's leading cricketers have featured in that tournament. So it was hardly a surprise when the local giant Mohammedan Sporting Club signed up Sanath along with Ranatunga. He was there to play just a couple of games, but his reputation preceded him.

Left-arm spinner Mohammed Rafique, who later played for Bangladesh, was a fan and fancied himself as a local Sanath. In fact, the local newspaper *Prothom Alo* famously dubbed Rafique as the 'Bangladeshi Jayasuriya'. Sanath even visited Rafique's home where he was shown the newspaper that had dubbed Rafique as his Bangladeshi clone.

Rafique used to strike big sixes while batting in the lower

middle-order in the Bangladesh domestic competitions, and he was gaining a major fan following. So, when Sanath came to Dhaka, Rafique gladly challenged him to test who had a better strike rate with the bat. With Sanath batting at the top of the order, he naturally had more opportunities to strike sixes than Rafique.

Sanath developed other friendships in Bangladesh, including a bond with their future captain Aminul Islam. Islam and Sanath had sparred against each other from the days of the inaugural Under-19 World Cup in 1988, and so, Islam was aware of Sanath's abilities. This was one of the main reasons why Mohammedan had signed him up.

This friendship helped Islam realize when Sanath would be unstoppable during batting. He faced this when Sanath smashed 108 against Bangladesh in an Asia Cup encounter in 1997 at Colombo, a few months after the Mohammedan stint.

Captain Akram Khan told Islam, the then vice-captain of the side, that he was bringing himself on the field. Akram was a rotund cricketer and not exactly agile on the field. He would bowl at a medium pace to save the day.

'When he told me that he wants to bowl, I did not want to disappoint him by discouraging him,' said Islam. Sanath tore Akram apart by taking him for 27 runs from the second over he bowled. 'After that he (Akram) never ever volunteered to bowl,' joked Islam. In fact, so scarred was Akram from the Sanath experience, that he bowled just twice more in his career. A decade later, Sanath even squared off against his nephew, Tamim Iqbal, just to underline his longevity as a cricketer.

Changing Gears, Yet Again

That effort during the Asia Cup was one of the many outstanding knocks in the calendar year of 1997 that Sanath played. His next major knock came at Lahore during a quadrangular tournament played to celebrate Pakistan's independence. Sri Lanka was returning to the city where they had been crowned the World Champion just one year ago. Hence, there was an air of confidence around them.

But what they dished out to Pakistan on a cold Lahore night— with dew all over Gaddafi Stadium—still has the locals talking. Sanath and de Silva, in particular, put the famed Pakistan bowling to sword in their chase for a stiff 280. They batted with such freedom that the chase was done in 40 overs as the stunned Pakistan team was booted out of their own celebrations. India had also suffered a similar fate in their tournament at the hands of Sanath.

But to see the likes of Wasim Akram, Waqar and Saqlain lost for ideas was something else. Sanath and de Silva added an unbeaten 213 runs for the third wicket. Even though Sri Lanka ended up losing the finals to South Africa, Sanath had managed to stamp his authority on the world stage yet again.

The year of 1997 was one of the most profitable years for Sanath as he logged more than 1000 runs in both Tests (1271 in 11 Tests) and ODIs (1178 in 26 games). This new-found consistency and superstar status landed him some endorsement deals with majors like Singer, Reebok and Pepsi. By this time, he was well and truly in the pantheon of Sri Lanka's revered champions.

There were, however, a few more battles to win.

Cricket has traditionally been a sport that was started by the Englishmen and appropriated by its former colonies. Showing their former masters that they were better than them was what drove most of the sides for a very long time. It certainly was the driving force for the champion West Indies sides of the 1960s, '70s and '80s. They played with an extra spring in their step and it resulted in some famous whitewashes.

In the case of Sri Lanka, there was similar motivation when they turned up to play against England. It was also because of the attitude of the English cricket team towards them. England had a policy whereby they would not entertain more than one Test against Sri Lanka either at home or away. The thinking in the Test and County Cricket Board (TCCB), as the England and Wales Cricket Board (ECB) was known earlier, was that Sri Lanka had to 'earn' their right to play against England in a full series (home or away).

The challenge for Sri Lanka was to beat England in a one-off Test in England so that they could finally gain the right to play a full series either at home or away. This was a slight that hurt many Sri Lankans.

Sri Lanka had toured England thrice before for one-off Tests in 1984, 1988 and 1991. Similarly, England had toured Sri Lanka only twice for one-off Tests in 1981–82 and then in 1992–93 when Ranatunga's men created history by beating them for the first time ever. But in the eyes of the mandarins of the cricket establishment at the Lord's, it was not enough. This was the reason why when the Arjuna Ranatunga-led Sri Lankan team reached England in the summer of 1998, there was a determination to prove their former masters wrong. That season in England turned out to be different.

After years of pouring scorn on Australia for their annual triangular competition in coloured clothing with white ball and black sight screens, England decided to finally embrace the concept at home. So, that summer in 1998 started with a full series of three

ODIs and five Tests against South Africa. Even before the tour had started, there was talk in the English county circuit amongst the professional cricketers about a man called Sanath Jayasuriya. When Saqlain joined Surrey County Cricket Club, based at The Oval, for the first time in 1997, he noticed some of his teammates and rivals only talking about Sanath. Having terrorized bowlers elsewhere, Sanath was a cause for worry to them.

For Sri Lanka, however, the tour started with the most tragic of circumstances, as they were out for a mere 54 in only their second game of the tour against Glamorgan. It seemed like the dream of showing the masters their worth would not be achieved even on that trip.

Sanath started the trip with an injury scare he received during a tour game against Kent. A spiteful pitch had ensured that a ball from Kent and England fast bowler Dean Headley hit his left index finger not once but four times. That game had to be stalled and a new one had to be scheduled as a replacement on a fresh pitch. There was a real chance of him missing a few games because of a broken finger. But he raced against time and was available for the bigger contests. However, he struggled with form throughout the triangular series.

The tide then began to turn as Ranatunga's men won the triangular competition, beating England in the final. The stage was now set for that tour finale—the one-off Test at the historic The Oval in London.

Whipping it up in Whites

In the English camp, however, the sights were already set elsewhere. There was limited time left for the side for the upcoming Ashes tour to Australia to be chosen. So, the hopefuls were already in Australia mentally.

'It was probably unfair on both sides to play that Test in hindsight. We had really had a tough five-Test series against South Africa including a nail-biter at Headingley. In our minds, the summer was already over by the time the Test against Sri Lanka came along. There was no disrespect; just our state of mind at the time,' recalled Mark Butcher, the England opener who featured in that Test, to the author.

The English team still managed to get organized and posted 445 in their first innings after being asked to bat first on what was a very dry brown Oval pitch. The move to insert England first by Ranatunga was criticized by many experts. England, however, was confident with the score. Having gone through a season of attrition cricket against the well-oiled South African side, most in the English side thought they had had enough.

'We thought we were safe,' Butcher recounted to the author.

In the ten Tests prior to the Oval contest, Sanath had scored five half-centuries but no centuries. In fact, since his blockbuster series against India in the August of 1997, it appeared as if he had gone off the boil. His tour form and the injury cloud before the Test further added to the mix. This uncertainty about Sanath really helped him as he rediscovered his mojo. 'Sanath came out and literally smoked us to all parts of the ground. There did not seem to be anything that could stop him,' Butcher remembered the knock.

He then allied with the elegant Aravinda de Silva. Together, the pair used various methods to destroy England's bowling. While Sanath was unconventional in his approach, de Silva was the attractive one who would kill softly. England's bowling combination of Dominic Cork, Darren Gough, Angus Fraser, Ian Salisbury and Ben Hollioake just did not know what hit them. Sanath and de Silva added 243 runs for the second in 325 balls, a pace that England was not used to in a Test. At one point, Butcher looked up to Fraser and said, 'We are never going to get these blokes out.' But they did, eventually.

Sanath finally fell for 213 off 278 balls in 346 minutes—his second double century in Test cricket with 33 boundaries and a six. De Silva, meanwhile, made a much more composed 152 off 292 deliveries. When the pair had finished, Sri Lanka had scored at such a rate that it afforded them enough opportunity to force an unlikely win.

Former West Indies fast bowler Michael Holding, now a reputed commentator in England, summed it up best: 'For nearly two days the England cricketers put the capacity crowd at the Surrey Oval to sleep. But on day three the brilliant batting display of the Sri Lankans—Sanath Jayasuriya, Aravinda de Silva and Arjuna Ranatunga—awoke the English spectators and set alight The Oval. What a fantastic performance by Sri Lankans.'[19]

The British papers, too, were full of praise for the pair, especially Sanath.

Writing in *The Telegraph*, celebrated cricket writer Scyld Berry praised the effort by likening Sanath's effort to the one and only Sir Donald Bradman:

The batting of Sri Lanka's master stroke players, Sanath Jayasuriya and Aravinda de Silva, has made England's cricket

---

[19]Premasara Epasinghe, 'Sanath, Aravinda and Arjuna Provided the Fireworks', cricinfo, 3 September 1998.

look small beer, or perhaps rice-water, by comparison.

Jayasuriya and de Silva came together when England made the costly mistake of dismissing Sri Lanka's No 3, caught in the gully off a loose drive. However fine a batsman Mahela Jayawardene may be, it is inconceivable he could have matched the virtuosity of the batsmanship which ensued, and kept on ensuing, until Jayasuriya had made a double hundred and Sri Lankan supporters in the crowd, deprived for so long of a sight of their team in this country for being 'unfashionable', were almost drunk on the rice-water of it all.

Perhaps no other pair of Test batsmen in the world could have batted so brilliantly and for so long at so rapid a rate. At the age of 29 the Sri Lankan left-hander is within reach of the consummation which a certain nonagenarian (Bradman) from Australia has alone achieved: that of scoring at a rate appropriate to one-day cricket with the certainty appropriate to a Test match.

Another venerable expert of the game, former Somerset captain and a writer par excellence, Peter Roebuck also gushed about Sanath in his column for *The Telegraph*.[20]

It was the great men of Sri Lankan cricket that took the day. Jayasuriya, the cricketing buccaneer, and Aravinda de Silva, previously rumbustious and now humble and settled.

Jayasuriya was magnificent. England could not contain him. In some respects he resembles Graeme Pollock for he, too, seems to grab the bat as much as hold it and he, too,

---

[20]Peter Roebuck, 'Murali Turns Gamble into Victory Chance', cricinfo, 30 August 1998.

waits ages for the ball before dispatching it with a plump of
the bottom hand.

The Sunday Times' much heralded cricket correspondent Simon
Wilde wrote:

> Jayasuriya and de Silva should rank among the world's most
> entertaining stroke-makers. Batting more like the one-day
> champions they are, that at a tempo familiar to Test audiences
> Sri Lanka challenged England's complacent thought of sending
> themselves off to Australia with three victories behind them
> by scoring 367 runs in a day for the loss of just two wickets.

Under a piece titled 'Imperious Jayasuriya shreds the dream team',
former England spinner Vic Marks wrote:

> It is a mark of Sri Lanka's current status in world cricket that
> none was in the least surprised when their batsmen elegantly
> shredded the England attack.

Sri Lanka finished their innings at 591 with a lead of 146 over
England. Despite all the praises for the Sanath-de Silva duo,
there was still the small matter of winning a Test match. At stake
was something bigger—the pride of Sri Lanka and the right to
play a full series against England. Then, the other star bowler of
Sri Lanka, Muttiah Muralitharan, took over. He spun through
England to claim figures of 9 for 65, to end with a match haul
of 16 for 220.

If Sanath and de Silva tired England, Murali delivered the
knockout punch with his trademark smile. Sanath then finished
the last rites to seal a famous win by 10 wickets for Sri Lanka.
The Old Blighty had finally been conquered. Sri Lanka could now

tour England by right for a full series and even host them at home with pride.

At the end of the Test match, left-handed Butcher, one of Murali's victims, reached out to one of his tribe, Sanath, to seek advice on how to play Murali. 'He said very easy, you (use your) pad, pad and then just cut. That's it,' said Butcher, which summed up Sanath's mindset as a batsman.

As luck would have it, Sanath led Sri Lanka when England visited Sri Lanka for their full tour of three Tests in 2000–01. Then, when Sri Lanka visited England in 2002 for a full tour, it was Sanath again who was leading the side. So, in his own way Sanath had broken the shackles of the past and had lived to tell the tale.

End of a Dream

However, in 1998–99, his form did not live up to the heights of 1996–98. He was now among the seniors of the side, with the likes of veteran Asanka Gurusinha retiring and another senior Mahanama struggling to retain his place.

There were other distractions along the way. The controversy over Murali's action flared up again leading to the now famous walkout led by Ranatunga during a tri-series match against England in Australia. At the same time, the strategy of going for a dash in the first 15 overs used in 1996 now had a counter from bowlers worldwide. Sri Lanka needed a fresh approach, but there was more confusion in the ranks. Yardley had been replaced by Sri Lanka's former batsman Roy Dias, while Mendis had been replaced as manager by Ranjit Fernando.

The lack of a strategy reflected most in the poor returns of Sanath in the 1999 World Cup. He scored just 82 runs from the five games Sri Lanka played. Sri Lanka's title defence failed as they crashed in the very first round. Even battered rivals like India's Venkatesh Prasad felt that the conditions in England offered him more confidence to deal with Sanath. 'Where the ball did a bit more, you felt comfortable in executing your plans against him. Like we showed during the World Cup, it was possible to keep him quiet there.'

An era in Sri Lankan cricket was about to end and Sanath was still unaware that he would spearhead the new era.

3

Sri Lanka and India

India and Sri Lanka have shared history. It is not just the
mythological association between the two countries, but in
the modern era too, there is a connection, thanks to migrant
Tamil labourers from India in Sri Lanka. The subsequent Indian
involvement in a peace mission in Sri Lanka following the LTTE
flare-up, the assassination of former Prime Minister Rajiv Gandhi
and the general politics surrounding the Tamil issue means that
both the countries have endured a lot together.

In cricket, too, the connection was somehow retained when
the Tamil Nadu Ranji team played an annual contest against the
Ceylon (as Sri Lanka was called earlier) national team for the M.J.
Gopalan Trophy. It was an annual contest that was staged regularly
till Sri Lanka attained Test status in 1981. Thereafter, it became
intermittent and now it has completely been stopped.

India exited the World Cups twice—first in 1979 and then

in 2007—thanks to Sri Lanka. The loss in 1979 was shocking as Sri Lanka was not yet a Test side. The loss in 2007 is much fresher because it led to a wave of outrage in India.

Despite these connections, cricketing ties between India and Sri Lanka in mid-1980s to early '90s were very weak. The 1983 World Cup-winning captain Kapil Dev led a side to Sri Lanka in 1985, which ended in a lot of acrimony. Umpiring decisions and aggressive crowd behaviour towards key Indian players like Mohammad Azharuddin in particular left Kapil's side exasperated. It seemed like Krishnamachari Srikkanth, possibly because of his Tamil roots, was the target of some biased umpiring. Due to these issues, India lost the Test series to Sri Lanka for the first time on that tour.

Kapil came back and ripped apart Sri Lankan cricket, pushing back the ties for a few years. India even boycotted the 1986 Asia Cup staged in Sri Lanka for that very reason. So, for the next few years, cricket exchanges between India and Sri Lanka came to a grinding halt.

Tryst With India Begins

But that era of Sri Lankan cricketers was ending and a new phase was beginning under Arjuna Ranatunga. Incidentally, Kapil was one of the first to take note of this as he picked his first-ever ODI hat-trick in the truncated 1990–91 Asia Cup final at Kolkata's Eden Gardens. Asia Cup that year was played without Pakistan, owing to the political troubles in Kashmir.

In the finals, Kapil claimed a unique hat-trick spread over two overs against Sri Lanka, which everyone took some time to realize. Kapil first got Roshan Mahanama to edge to keeper Kiran More off the ball of his previous over. Off the first ball of his next over, a young man named Sanath, then a middle-order batsman who bowled a bit of left-arm spin, skied the ball and Sanjay Manjrekar held on to it. Batsmen crossed and Rumesh Ratnayake was trapped leg-before to give Kapil his first hat-trick.

But on that day at Eden Gardens, there was a spectator, Abhishek Mukherjee (former chief editor of cricketcountry.com), who saw Sanath in action for the first time and felt that he had seen something special even in that brief knock.

Years later, Mukherjee said to the author:

The inclusion of Jayasuriya in the Sri Lankan side was somewhat mysterious: he had batted at number five on ODI debut, and had never batted at anywhere above number six again. Coming into the tournament, his nine ODIs had fetched him 76 runs at 10.85 and a strike rate of 49. Not that he bowled, he sent down a mere 3 overs. Along with many other ardent fans of the sport, I was confused over his selection. It was my first sighting of Sanath. Here, too, he scored a mere 5, but the runs were historically significant: he played a trademark short-arm cut before flicking one off his legs. Just over five years from the innings, bowlers across the world would be terrorized by Jayasuriya executing exactly the same two strokes.

For the next couple of years, India and Sri Lanka drifted apart in cricketing relations, after which normal services were about to resume. Sanath came to the fore when Mohammed Azharuddin led a side in July 1993 to Sri Lanka for the first full series there since the controversy-ridden tour of 1985.

The Indian cricket team really sat up and took notice of Sanath the batsman when they started the tour with a three-day tour match—a warm-up fixture—before the actual series got underway against a Sri Lankan Board President's XI at the Welagedara Stadium, Kurunegala, a town just off Colombo.

That side, led by future captain Hashan Tillakaratne, had a number of players who would go on to play with distinction for Sri Lanka much later. The other players included openers Chandika Hathurusingha, Dulip Samaraweera, Marvan Atapattu, wicketkeeper Romesh Kaluwitharana, paceman Ravindra Pushpkumara and spinner Ruwan Kalpage. In most cases, such tour matches are a footnote when the actual series ends. But in the case of this tour match, there was one man who stayed in the minds of Indians. Not just the ones who played in that match, but also those in the travelling media contingent.

'We had been told by the local press that there is this left-hander from Matara...a crazy fellow. He is known to play some astounding, outrageous shots,' recalled Vijay Lokapally, currently deputy sports editor at *The Hindu*, but on tour at the time in 1993.

And that man was Sanath. He walked out to bat at number six with his side struggling at 97 for 4. And by the time he had finished, he had struck 151 off 239 balls. That innings left an impression on the Indians because he struck 21 boundaries and a towering six.

'Usually Sri Lankans had attractive stroke-makers like Aravinda (de Silva), Roy Dias till then. They would occupy the crease by playing correct strokes. But this guy was different. We had already picked up all the top-order batsmen. So nobody expected that he would come in at number six and smash us all over. That set us thinking about his potential,' recalled former India left-arm spinner Venkatpathy Raju who actually ended Sanath's blitzkrieg in the match.

Sanath especially impressed the Indian Captain Azharuddin. 'Azhar used to write his syndicated columns with me at the time and he kept saying, "This guy (Sanath) is tremendous; where should we bowl to him?"' recalled Lokapally to the author.

Another Indian cricketer, wicketkeeper Kiran More, kept to Sanath in that tour game and he still cannot get over what he calls his 'cow-boy approach' in that knock. So, while the rest of the world had a year to hear about his first big effort in an international arena, the Indian team had already borne the brunt of his aggression once. India did play against Sri Lanka in five more ODIs before the 1996 World Cup, and by then, Sanath had moved up the order. But he hardly ever crossed half-century in any of those games.

However, a shot in one of the games in a quadrangular in Sri Lanka in 1994 left one Indian player, Venkatesh Prasad, gasping for breath. For a major part of his career, Sanath hammered Prasad quite mercilessly, but that day in 1994, Prasad was in awe of him.

'I still remember he swept Kapil. Now Kapil was a legend, who had obviously dropped his pace, but to hit him like that, for me was unbelievable. I was standing at deep square-leg and wondering where has this guy (Sanath) come from,' recalled Prasad to the author.

With that background, it was hardly a surprise that Sanath became quite a dasher when Ranatunga and the new coach Dav Whatmore gave him the licence. He also had Romesh Kaluwitharna for company, especially in the ODIs.

In a New Light

By the time India played against Sri Lanka again in the 1996 World Cup, the face of Sri Lankan cricket had changed. India was obviously not prepared for it. Sri Lanka travelled to New Delhi for the first away game of that tournament against their co-host. It was a gloomy day in February 1996 with thick smog covering the sky above the Feroz Shah Kotla Ground. The game itself started with a slight delay of about 15 minutes because of the smog. When India batted, the entire stadium was delirious as Sachin Tendulkar slammed yet another century in that tournament.

There was a brief 10-minute rain break when India batted (in the 39th over), but the game quickly resumed and all seemed in order. The Indian team felt that they had enough runs (271–3) on the board and were confident of just running away with it.

'We always had better of them in those days. So we thought it would be enough. In those days anything above 250 was enough,' Prasad later recounted to the author. Sitting out of the match, Raju, too, felt the same as Sri Lanka started their now-famous chase.

Up against Sanath was Manoj Prabhakar, a man who had given him enough trouble early in his career. 'He was one of the most difficult bowlers I faced early in my career because of the swing he could get,' Sanath remembered.[21]

Then thirty-three years old, Prabhakar was a Delhi boy who was rated as a street fighter. He never possessed great pace, but his guile with the ball was what brought him success. He would open the batting and bowling, so in many ways, he was a unique all-rounder.

But that day, everything went haywire. Sanath, and then Kaluwitharwarna, took 33 off Prabhakar's first 2 overs. India sat up and watched in shock. There was pin-drop silence at the Kotla

---

[21]Interview by Nagraj Gollapudi, 'I'd Like to Play for Another Six Months', ESPNcricinfo, 27 December 2009.

Stadium as Indians saw Sanath's fury for the first time.

'The highlight for me was getting a lot of runs against Prabhakar. We made 50 in the first 4 overs and most of the runs I made against Prabhakar. But on that day, I felt really nice and I didn't want to stop,' Sanath told ESPNcricinfo.[22]

Prabhakar was packed off, only to return later to bowl two more overs for 14 runs, only this time he was bowling off-spin! Sanath had reduced the man to a sorry state. Prabhakar was booed off the ground in his own city—a sight no one can ever forget. He finished a bitter man, never to play for India at any level again. Prabhakar, in an oblique way, extracted revenge from Sanath in a few years' time.

In the Indian dressing room, there was complete silence as they watched with shock how Sanath was dealing with the other bowlers too. Raju ran in with advice from Ajit Wadekar (cricket manager) at times, but they could do nothing that day.

Wicketkeeper Nayan Mongia was seen running to bowlers, shouting advices to them. 'That day he appeared so confident… nothing worked for us. Manoj was a great swing bowler, who had to try something different, so he bowled spin. We realized a lot of things about this guy (Sanath) that day and learnt how to bowl to him in future.'

Eventually, things did pick up when Anil Kumble snared a few wickets, but the pace set by Sanath was such that Sri Lanka was never in a hurry. Despite being scarred by the defeat in New Delhi, India eventually made it to the semi-finals. They made it to that stage after beating Pakistan in the quarter-final at Bengaluru. India was now headed to Calcutta to take on Sri Lanka in the semi-final, in what appeared to be a grudge match. All the energy was focused

---

[22]Ibid.

on dismissing Sanath and his partner at an early stage. India did succeed, but then the team took their eyes off the ball.

Former batsman Sanjay Manjrekar spelt out the problem in the Indian camp in his autobiography, *Imperfect*:[23]

> Before the semi-final against Sri Lanka, (Indian cricket manager Ajit) Wadekar called for a team meeting. It went on for quite long; Wadekar did most of the talking. Once he was done, Mohammad Azharuddin, the captain, spoke a few words. Although that meeting lasted an hour or so, around fifty minutes were spent on how to contain their openers Romesh Kaluwitharana and Sanath Jayasuriya.
>
> Imagine our surprise, then, when we got both out in the first over in the semi-final. Now we didn't know what to do. Like Abhimanyu in *Mahabharata*, we had trained ourselves to get to the target in the 'chakravyuh' but didn't prepare ourselves about getting out of it.
>
> If you look at our jubilation after getting Kaluwitharana and Jayasuriya out, it was as if we had won the World Cup. We basically took the eye off the ball, and Aravinda de Silva made us pay for it. Sri Lanka ended up scoring 251.

India's chase ended in flames as after Tendulkar and Manjrekar fell, the spinners of Sri Lanka, including Sanath, spun a web. When the match finally ended, owing to crowd disturbance, a billion hearts were broken. The image of a teary-eyed Vinod Kambli walking off is still fresh in everyone's minds. India had been humbled in their own backyard. Sri Lanka finally arrived in the consciousness of the Indian fan's mind.

---

[23]Sanjay Manjrekar, *Imperfect*, HarperCollins, 20 December 2017.

Very few international cricketers had managed to capture the attention of the Indian public. Among those in that shortlist were great West Indies all-rounder Sir Garfield Sobers and former international captains, the charismatic pair of Imran Khan and Sir Viv Richards. Now there was one Sri Lankan, Sanath, who too had risen through the ranks to be seen as a superstar in his own right.

To understand how Sanath had arrived, you had to hear the rumour-mongering fixated on him at the time. Some alleged that there was a spring in Sanath's bat, which enabled him to bat the way he did against India. 'As a bowler, you sort of wanted to believe that (rumour) to feel good about bowling to him,' Raju joked with the author many years later.

India did play against Sri Lanka a few more times in 1996. Sanath was often snapped up by his usual foe Srinath, but he did slam his first century in ODI cricket against India in one of the many tournaments played in that era.

Much in Demand

Sanath was now in very high demand in India and was now being accepted as one of India's own. In November 1996, nearly eight months after he first exploded on the scene, Sanath was being chased by the glitzy world of Mumbai. He first teamed up with his dashing partner Kaluwitharna for a fund-raising double-wicket tournament for Mumbai's Ruia College, at the Wankhede Stadium. Also taking part in the contest were the senior Lankan pair of de Silva and Ranatunga. The tournament also included Tendulkar, Kambli, Robin Singh, Srinath, Kumble and Rahul Dravid. De Silva and Ranatunga edged out Sanath and Kaluwitharna by 4 runs. Sanath was easily the second-best batsman, after de Silva, in course of the day-night fixture as he smashed 12 sixes and 10 boundaries.

While Sanath was in Mumbai, he was to don the grease paint too. He was signed up by fashion major Pantaloons as one of the international cricketers to model for the brand.

Sanath was to join the likes of the Waugh twins Steve and Mark, disgraced late South African captain Hansie Cronje and all-rounder Brian McMillan in the Pantaloons ads. The company had consciously decided to keep away from Indian cricketers because they were proving to be too costly.

'You ask me why we don't take Indian cricketers for modelling our clothes, and I'll tell you that it's because they are too expensive,' said Rakesh Biyani, founder and director of Pantaloon Fashions (India) Ltd.[24]

Jury is Out

Just days after that, in the same month (November 1996), India hosted the Miss World beauty pageant for the first and last time. It was staged at the M. Chinnaswamy Cricket Stadium in Bengaluru. The man behind the pageant was India's Hindi film superstar, Amitabh Bachchan, who was finding his way back into the mainstream after years of exile. He had launched his own company, Amitabh Bachchan Corporation Limited (ABCL), and was hoping to enter the big league with this venture. But the pageant faced a lot of issues from extreme elements of the state of Karanataka and

---

[24]Lankans Dominate in Double-Wicket Tourney, Sony ESPN, 18 November 1996.

was staged under immense duress. Bachchan staked his personal reputation in conducting the event.

Bachchan was personally involved in picking the pool of judges. Sanath was playing an ODI tournament in Nairobi two months before that, when he received the invitation to be part of the elite panel.

'I simply said yes. I had no idea why I had been chosen, but I guess cricket had a lot to do with it!' he recalled days later in an interview to Sri Lanka's *The Sunday Times*.[25]

Before leaving to judge the competition, Sanath decided to seek the advice of a female friend in Colombo who worked at an advertising firm. He arrived four days before the event, but got involved in a string of pre-pageant parties. Sanath was now in a world of glitz and glamour. Just twelve months ago, this had been unknown to him. But this was the extent to which his life had changed since the 1996 World Cup heroics.

He was now sitting alongside a number of achievers from across the world, including India's matinee idol Aamir Khan and Miss World 1994 Aishwarya Rai. On the actual day, Sanath was seated to the left of Aishwarya and Aamir. Also part of the panel was the now disgraced businessman Vijay Mallya. The other judges of the panel were Andre Sekulic, Linda Pétursdóttir (Miss World 1988 from Iceland), Marlene Cardin, Ninibeth Leal (Miss World 1991, Venezuela), Tom Nuyens (Mister World 1996, Belgium) and late socialite Parmeshwar Godrej.

It is worth mentioning these two names from the panel because the Indian pair and Sanath were the most sought after by the fans.

---

[25]'No Maidens for Sanath', The Sunday TimesPlus, http://www.sundaytimes.lk/961208/plusm.html#Sanath, 8 December 1996.

With a virtual lockdown due to various extremist organization threats, Bengaluru was a cauldron of sorts at that time. There had been threats of mass suicides, but all the drama was happening away from the centre of the city where Sanath and the judges were staying at the Windsor Manor.

'Aamir, Aishwarya and I were supposedly in need of the most security, but we managed with one guard each. My friend and I even managed to slip out and go shopping by ourselves,' Sanath recalled later in an interview to *The Sunday Times*.[26]

He was mobbed during the shopping trip by cricket fans who recognized him instantly. But it was very quickly down to business for him. The judges had to first meet with the chairman of the Miss World Organization, Eric Morley, who briefed them about the process of judging and the various rounds.

Then, the 88 contestants (minus the mysterious absentee Miss Sri Lanka) individually spoke to the judges for about three minutes. In some cases, the contestants were not English-speaking, so the process of having an interpreter by their side was time-consuming.

'I basically asked them what they would do if they won the title, how they would go about getting aid for the needy children of the world and what they would do for their countries by way of charity and so on. Whereas the poise and figure of a participant were deemed very important in addition to personality, beauty was only an added benefit and not something to focus on,' Sanath said.[27] The judges, however, could not mingle with the contestants during leisure periods.

---

[26]Ibid.
[27]Ibid.

On the day of the competition, people back home in Sri Lanka saw the competition live on their television screens. They saw their boy having an animated discussion with Aishwarya Rai.

'I thought all the judges were very nice,' he said. 'Aamir Khan, Mr World from Belgium, Aishwarya...all of them. We really didn't get to talk on a personal basis though, since we met on such few occasions....'[28]

When the hosts for the evening, American actor Richard Steinmetz and Canadian-born Ruby Bhatia, began introducing the judges for the night, there was a huge applause. As expected, some of the loudest cheers were for Aamir and Aishwarya, but the adulation for Sanath was equally loud. The event was held in a cricket stadium after all—somewhere Sanath had played two years ago in a Test against India. When Bhatia called out his name, Sanath gave a nervous smile as he waved to the large crowd. It was this moment that made him feel as if he was facing the first ball of a Test match.

As the event raced along, he was the happiest because most of the contestants he had voted for made it to the final stage. 'It does look like I have good taste in women!' he jokingly proclaimed to sum up a night to remember.[29] India had truly embraced him, making him the first Sri Lankan poster boy. 'It was nice to represent Sri Lanka at something, for the first time ever. I am proud and honoured to have been chosen.'[30]

---

[28]Ibid.
[29]Ibid.
[30]Ibid.

Making Life Hell

Sanath returned to India in April 1997 for what was the 50th anniversary of our independence. India played against Sri Lanka in Mumbai during that tournament and posted a modest 225 for 7. Before the game, India had their usual team meeting under the new captain Sachin Tendulkar. The focus of Tendulkar and Coach Madan Lal's speech was on not giving any width to Sanath. Even though Mumbai paceman Abey Kuruvilla was playing against Sanath for the first time, he was aware of all his exploits over the past twelve months.

'We had removed Kalu early and were looking for that one breakthrough to get back in that match,' recalled Kuruvilla. But that breakthrough never came. Sanath went berserk at the Wankhede Stadium as he smashed an unbeaten 151 off 120 balls with 17 boundaries and 4 sixes.

Tendulkar spent what was the first of many games in 1997 running to his bowlers and exhorting them to keep their heads high. But nothing seemed to work that day in his beloved home ground. Sanath scored a lion's share in the chase and sealed it quite easily.

Cricket in general and Indian cricket in particular had not embraced technology. So there were no analysts providing footage and data to the bowlers on what they needed to do against a batsman like Sanath. The bowlers depended a lot on the trial and error method to work things out.

As a result, bowlers of that era, especially Prasad, admitted to losing confidence when bowling to Sanath. India needed the services of their premier fast bowler Javagal Srinath, a destroyer of medium-pace bowling. Sanath feared Srinath the most and had made that known in many interviews since his 1996 World Cup exploits. Unfortunately, by the time India played Sri Lanka again, Srinath was rendered hors de combat with a shoulder injury, having been bowled to the ground. Thus, India engaged in a battle against Sri Lanka, in Sri Lanka, without their major weapon. Sanath was licking his lips in anticipation.

The Marathon Man

As per custom, India lost the Asia Cup to Sri Lanka in the finals and all hopes now rested on the two-Test series that were to follow. Both sides had not played a Test since January 1994. India hoped that a change of format would result in a change of result.

India entered the Test series with five regular bowlers, hoping to enforce a result on what was touted to be a flat R. Premadasa Stadium pitch in the heart of Colombo. India batted first and by the end of the second day, posted what seemed like a reasonable 537 for 8. With three centurions in Navjot Sidhu (111), Tendulkar (143) and Azharuddin (126), India seemed to have control on the match.

Sri Lanka had pushed along to 39 when Tendulkar threw the ball to debutant left-arm spinner Nilesh Kulkarni. Both hailed from Mumbai and Tendulkar felt it was the right time to introduce Kulkarni into the attack.

The trick worked as Kulkarni snared Atapattu off his very first ball in Test cricket, caught behind by Mongia. India and Kulkarni celebrated like never before because they were on track now. Kulkarni had become the first Indian bowler ever to claim a wicket off his first ball in Test cricket.

Both the squads returned to the hotel, Taj Samudra, at the

end of the second day. Kulkarni was greeted by a smiling Muttiah Muralitharan, the Sri Lankan magician. 'Congrats macha, but good luck for the next three days,' Murali told Kulkarni with a smile, leaving the Mumbaikar confused. Little did Kulkarni know that Murali probably knew what was in store.

On the third day, Indians bowled, bowled and bowled. Sanath, now joined in by his good friend Roshan Mahanama, batted, batted and batted. There was just no stopping. They bided their time, mixing caution with aggression. Indians had gone wicketless, but had convinced themselves that the tide would turn after Sri Lanka ended the third day at 322 for 1.

'We had seen wicketless days in domestic cricket especially with Delhi and Tamil Nadu batting. So we tried to motivate ourselves somehow,' recalled Kulkarni to the author. In the dressing room, Coach Madan Lal kept hoping for that one wicket, but it just would not come.

When the teams returned to the hotel, Sanath still seemed fresh as ever. He met his journalist friend from India, Lokapally of *The Hindu*, as they both waited to get their keys from the receptionist. 'Just ask him (Lokapally) what's the score today?' Sanath joked with the receptionist after coming back unbeaten at 175. Lokapally later recalled this to the author.

Sanath was batting like a man possessed. It was not like a man who bludgeons the bowling in ODIs. This was someone different—it was like someone who was prepared to play the waiting game. That surprised the Indian team even more.

The other aspect of his innings was when he tried to take his own time to complete his routines while batting. He would first make a mark with the bat on the crease, then touch his pad, thigh pad and look around. This whole routine got to Prasad.

In a bid to hurry Sanath and in the hope of breaking his concentration, Prasad ran onto bowl even before he was ready. Sanath would have backed off, but the idea was to try and do something different.

'The worst thing is having to wait after being thrashed. I even complained to the umpires because it was getting on my nerves. That's the reason I tried a different tactic of running in even as he was getting ready, but sadly even that did not work,' Prasad recalled to the author.

India just did not have any answer. They tried eight bowlers in all, but all were left hanging high and dry. Kulkarni now realized why Murali had wished him good luck. The closest Kulkarni came to negating Murali's wishes was when a huge leg-before appeal against Sanath off his bowling was turned down. Kulkarni went wicketless for the remainder of the Test match, forcing the team manager Professor Ratnakar Shetty to coin a joke—'First ball wonder ball, rest all thunder ball.'

Sometime on the fourth day, the Indian team felt Sri Lanka could have declared and pushed for a result, but there was no such indication from Ranatunga. Both Sanath and Mahanama added 548 runs for the second wicket by the time the fourth day ended at 587 for one. Sanath had reached an unbeaten 326, while Mahanama was batting on 211.

Sanath and Mahanama had batted for two full days to compile the highest partnership for any wicket, surpassing the 467 set by the New Zealand pair of Andrew Jones and Martin Crowe for the third wicket against Sri Lanka in 1991. Sanath and Mahanama joined the company of West Indies greats, Sir Garfield Sobers and Sir Frank Worrell, who had batted for two days against England in the Barbados Test of 1959–60.

The Sri Lankan pair, however, outscored Sobers and Worrell, who put on 165 on the fourth day and 207 on the fifth. Sanath-Mahanama added 283 runs on the third day and another 265 on the fourth day. Their friendship grew stronger during that stand. Mahanama was under a lot of pressure to retain his place in the playing XI and that knock went a long way in saving him the axe.

'Roshan and I are very close, we were friends in any case,' reminisced Sanath later in a chat with *Wisden India*. 'Day in and day out, we were together most of the time. Playing with him was like home, it was like I was playing with my brother kind of thing. It was a very natural feeling, there wasn't any sort of fear or pressure. As a senior player, he gave me a lot of confidence but at that time, I was in too good a form. It was kind of a homely feeling playing alongside Roshan. Even though we were playing in Sri Lanka, playing with him was like a family thing, that kind of a feeling—if you know what I am saying.'[31]

'During our partnership, we spoke mostly of cricket, I am fairly sure, because he also wanted to prove himself, that he was worth his place. And for me to get a big 300 is something that I had never given any thought to. That was the key for me to get a 300—till I passed 250, I never felt that I would get 300. And it is only after you actually get to 300 that you feel you have done something special.'

But not more than 3,000 spectators were watching this contest. The gates were opened only on the final day, as Sanath was just 50 runs behind West Indies champion Brian Lara's, who had a world record score of 375.

'I have always wanted to play a long Test innings, so this one made me very happy,' a tired Sanath said at the end of the fourth

---

[31]Wisden India (the website shut down in July 2018).

day. 'It's an honour to be the highest scorer for Sri Lanka. I have been told of Lara's record. But I am too tired to think of it now.'[32]

Only three years and 110 days before this Sanath marathon, Lara had snatched Sobers' 36-year-old world record of 365 against England in 1994. Faraway in Port of Spain, Trinidad and Tobago, Lara himself was bracing to lose the record. 'It's not going to be a sad moment,' Lara said on TV 6 in an interview. 'Anybody who holds a world record would like to hold it for a very long time. But I'm not going to be sad for the occasion, I'm going to be happy for him (Sanath).'[33]

But Lara knew better than anyone else that returning to the crease would be the toughest task for Sanath. 'Three years ago, the last 46 were the hardest I ever had to score. There are going to be a lot of anxious moments tomorrow (today). But I think how his confidence is, how his mind is will determine whether or not he does it.'[34]

There was an air of expectation at the Premadasa Stadium as 30,000 people turned up on the final day and the gates were opened up to allow the free entry of spectators. Lara, too, wished Sanath luck. 'I am wishing him all the best. He is a nice player to see play. And he has just got to put his head down and play the same way he has been playing for the last couple days.'

Considering the ten-hour time difference between Trinidad and Tobago and Sri Lanka, Lara was unaware of what happened to Sanath the following day as he was fast asleep when the match began in Colombo. But just about 25 minutes into the start of the

[32]'Lara's 375 Under Threat', *Trinidad Express*, 7 August 1997.
[33]Ibid.
[34]Ibid.

match, Mahanama fell for 225 to Kumble. At that time, Mahanama felt he should have stayed on to help Sanath achieve the milestone. 'I was disappointed I had let Sanath down when I got out. I thought I should have stayed there to help him achieve the world record,' he said.[35]

In the very next over, Sanath was dismissed for 340 off a very tame shot, caught at silly point by Sourav Ganguly off Rajesh Chauhan. Sri Lankan Captain Ranatunga also sensed this could happen because he had advised Mahanama to hang on until Sanath reached his landmark.

'Most of us were keen to see Sanath break the world record. The players and the manager (Mendis) were more worried and nervous than Sanath on the final morning. What I told Roshan was to try and stay till Sanath breaks the record because we knew that when a partnership breaks automatically, the other person might get out,' said Ranatunga.[36] There was an air of despondency on the ground. Every Indian player ran to wish Sanath as he finished 35 short of Lara's record.

'Even though I had batted for so long, or maybe because of that and the fact that (Brian Lara's) record was very close, there was a little bit of tightness in the body and mind. If I had to go through that again, I would have done things a lot differently. I would have been more relaxed. I would have been calmer, I wouldn't want to think the way I did then. Everyone wanted me to get there, it was like a must-do thing, non-negotiable. And that really got to me,' Sanath later said to the author.

---

[35]Sa'adi Thawfeeq, 'Tendulkar Critical of Test Pitch', ESPNcricinfo, 8 August 1997.
[36]Ibid.

It was quite late in the night in Port of Spain, Trinidad and Tobago, so Lara had to be woken up by a family member to let him know that his record was safe. He had a restful 24 hours not knowing whether he would still hold the record for the highest individual Test score.

'When the record looked threatened, I felt that if he (Sanath) broke it, then I would be spurred on to greater things. But getting to 340 is close enough! And it is certainly a wake-up call for me to put it beyond the reach of everyone,' Lara told *The Trinidad Express*. Lara did live up to his promise and has since put it beyond everyone by bettering his 375 with a score of 400 in 2004 against England.

The Test also marked the debut of another great Sri Lankan batsman, Mahela Jayawardene. But the moment and the Test belonged to Sanath. In all, the match yielded 1,489 runs and a mere 14 wickets. Sri Lanka, at 952 for six, also eclipsed England's 903 for 7 declared against Australia at The Oval, which had stood as Test cricket's highest team total since 1938. The Sanath-Mahanama partnership record was broken almost a decade later by another Sri Lankan pair, Kumar Sangakkara and Mahela Jayawardene. That effort in 2006 against South Africa, however, did not quite carry the same legendary status.

But not everyone was happy with the outcome of the contest in 1997. The pitch in particular was a subject of special criticism amongst Indian bowlers, especially the medium-pacers Prasad and Kuruvilla—'It was like a concrete road.'

West Indies' celebrated late broadcaster Tony Cozier was one of them as he wrote a critical review of the Test from Colombo in the British newspaper *The Independent*.

In a match already wallowing in an ocean of runs and

records, the most coveted standard of all eluded their left-handed opener, Sanath Jayasuriya, on the final day of the first Test against India, but Sri Lanka still had the satisfaction of surpassing a mark of far longer standing.

It was irrelevant to the Test as a genuine contest, but the 30,000 afforded free admission principally to witness Jayasuriya reach his goal and packed into the Premadasa Stadium were exultant. It was a further psychological fillip to Sri Lanka's status as undisputed champions of the one-day game.

On the first four days of the match no more than 3,000 spectators were in the ground and it was only Jayasuriya's proximity to Lara's mark and the open gates that attracted a full house on the final day. The crowd had come in their droves, carrying their drums, trumpets and flags—and their hopes and expectations. For most it was a mere formality for the popular Jayasuriya to add the 50 runs he needed to take his place at the head of the game's most illustrious batting list.

Sri Lanka could claim superiority but did it really amount to much?

At the end of the Test match, an exhausted Tendulkar put Sanath on a pedestal. 'I have not seen Don Bradman bat, but I have seen Sanath Jayasuriya. I have not seen a better batsman in my cricketing career,' Tendulkar praised Sanath in his post-Test comments.[37]

Tendulkar paid rich tributes to Sanath immediately after the Test ended in a post-match press conference.

---

[37]Interview by Nagraj Gollapudi, 'I'd Like to Play for Another Six Months', http://www.espncricinfo.com/magazine/content/story/441258.html, 27 December 2009.

It was a new side of Sanath Jayasuriya we saw. He is known for going after the bowling, but on this occasion he showed a lot of patience and different character altogether. I wouldn't want to take away the credit from Sanath and Roshan because it requires a lot of courage to bat for two days. It is a very, very difficult task in Test cricket to bat for two days. Not many guys in the world have done it.[38]

However, Tendulkar raised questions, much like Cozier, on whether Sri Lanka should have pushed for a win. 'Records are meant to be broken, but your focus should be to win the game. If records are broken automatically, that's fine, but I wouldn't ask anybody from my team to go for any particular record. We are here to win and not break records,' said Tendulkar.[39]

A tired Sanath turned up for the post-match press conference and flatly denied that he or the side was focused on the Lara record or the highest team total.

We never thought about any records. Our first aim was to avert the follow-on. We got to know about the record when we came for tea on the fourth day when Arjuna said that we were some nine runs away from it. At that point only, we got to know we were in sight of a world record. It was a good opportunity for me to break the world record score of 375, but I didn't actually have it in mind. It was very hard to concentrate especially on the fourth day after lunch. The ball from Chauhan (that got him out) bounced a bit more than I expected.

[38]Sa'adi Thawfeeq, 'Tendulkar Critical of Test Pitch', ESPNcricinfo, 8 August 1997.
[39]Ibid.

Sanath had scarred Indian cricket forever and it would take a long time for the Indian team to recover from that shock. That Test match, however, led to a spate of jokes surrounding the Indian team. There was one where a passenger reaches the airport and is confronted by the customs officer.

Customs officer: Anything to declare?
Passenger: Yes sir, the Sri Lankan innings.

Sanath had left quite an impact on the Indian team. So when the second and final Test started not far away from the Premadasa Stadium at the Sinhalese Sports Club, India prayed for a change of luck because the pitch promised to be juicier. They did get Sanath out cheaply in the first innings for 32, but in the second, normal service resumed.

There were numerous rain interruptions in the second Test. At one point, as the match resumed after a rain break and the players came back onto the field, Ajay Jadeja decided to have some fun. He created a circle and joked about doing some black magic in it. Sanath saw this and walked around it, so as to avoid the spell. There were smiles all around with this charade, but it conveyed the deep impact of his batting.

He scored a 199 in the second Test and when he was clean bowled by Kuruvilla, the Mumbaikar was left surprised. 'I raised my hand and wondered whether I have actually taken his wicket! It was almost as if he was tired of hitting us,' Kuruvilla recalled to the author.

Throughout the second Test, the weather in Colombo was oppressively humid, coupled with Sanath's breathtaking batting. This led to a slowdown and India was later fined—100 per cent of their match fee—by the ICC match-referee John Reid of New

Zealand for slow over-rate in the Test. The substitute fielder Vinod Kambli wondered where the delay was. 'I got your drinks, pads, gloves on time during all breaks. Why should I be paying the fine?' he joked with his teammates. This was later recounted to the author.

Sanath ended with 571 runs from the two-Test series, bettering Englishman Wally Hammond's tally of 563 for a two-Test series in 1932–33 against New Zealand. Sanath went on to score just one more century (111) against India in Test cricket and that came in a winning cause as captain in 2001 at Galle. But his Test record against India was always going to be about the exploits of 1997 under the hot sun in Colombo.

But when the climate changed and got a bit cooler, India seemed to have the wood over him. In the 1999 World Cup staged in England, for example, the Indian bowlers seemed confident while dealing with Sanath. He got out cheaply, mainly because the bowlers felt they would not be defeated by the conditions, like in the subcontinent.

As expected, his exploits in ODI cricket against India continued to hurt in the subcontinent. Of his seven ODI hundreds against India, perhaps the most impactful was his knock of 189 in the Sharjah Champions Trophy finals in 2000 as the captain of Sri Lanka. India was reeling under the after-effects of match-fixing. A new captain in Ganguly was leading a new-look side, but it seemed Sanath was not keen for any mercy.

He smashed 189 off 161 balls with 21 boundaries and 4 sixes in a total of 299 for 5. The next best score was Russell Arnold's 52. Prasad was one of the lone survivors of his brutal assault from the 1990s, and felt a sense of déjà vu as he bowled to him that day in Sharjah.

'It was a typical knock with shots over points, over square leg.

He would be severe on anything slightly loose. I did not have a clue after a point because he was that good that day,' said Prasad, who gave away 73 runs from his 7 overs.

So severe was the impact that India just could not get going and were bowled out for a mere 54, only to hand Sri Lanka a famous 245-run victory. Sanath won the Best Batsman, Best Fielder, Fastest 50, Most Sixes, Man of the Match, and finally, Man of the Series awards post the finals.

'We have played as a team throughout the tournament and that is why we have won all four games. It has been fantastic and I would like to thank all the players for being so supportive,' said a beaming Sanath to the author, after the finals.

Cricket in a Fix

Around this time, the unfinished Prabhakar story was starting to rear its head. Prabhakar famously ran an anti-corruption plank in Indian cricket, leading to several heads rolling, including that of Azhar, Jadeja and Ajay Sharma. Prabhakar even accused Kapil of offering him money to throw a match against Pakistan in 1994. He was reportedly offered US$500,000 to fix matches by an Indian bookie, Mukesh Gupta. The arrest of Gupta was after a series of exposes by Prabhakar. This was followed by the downfall of the former South African captain, the late Hansie Cronje in April 2000 when he admitted to links with bookies.

Gupta had told India's Central Bureau of Investigation (CBI) that he approached Sanath in Dubai in 1996, after the World Cup triumph. The incident was mentioned in CBI's 162-page report on match-fixing. It was later revealed that Sanath had told the BCCSL officials about this offer.

'Several attempts were made to get to Sanath but none of them did,' a former Sri Lankan Cricket Board official was quoted as saying by *The Sunday Times*. 'One big offer was made to him in Dubai but Sanath told the bookie in plain terms to get lost. Sanath told several people about it. He told me, he told everybody here. Even Gupta admitted he was unsuccessful.'[40]

The Sunday Times also claimed that Sanath along with Mahanama and Asanka Gurusinha were approached during the 1992 Australian tour of Sri Lanka by some Indian bookies to leak information about the match. Delhi-based Gupta claimed to have paid money to a number of international cricketers, including England's Alec Stewart, Sanath's teammates Ranatunga and Aravinda de Silva, but all denied Gupta's claims.

The ICC had then constituted an Anti-Corruption Unit (ACU) headed by Lord Paul Condon. As part of its remit, Sanath, de Silva and Ranatunga were to be interviewed by Condon and ACU investigator Jeff Rees in April 2001. The Sri Lankan board had set up its own inquiry headed by noted human rights lawyer Desmond Fernando. Later in July 2001, Fernando submitted a report clearing all the players.

Sanath put all this behind him and continued tormenting India for a few more years. He had 3 more ODI hundreds against India. In 2004, he slammed a century in the Asia Cup just when questions rose about his place in the XI.

But the knock that is still rated highly came in the 2008 edition of Asia Cup in Karachi when he had just turned 39. He played the

---

[40] Charlie Austin, 'Jayasuriya to be Quizzed by Condon's Anti-corruption Team', ESPNcricinfo, http://www.espncricinfo.com/ci/content/story/99680.html?wrappertype=print, 25 February 2001.

lone ranger as he smashed 125 off 114 balls with 9 boundaries and 5 sixes. Sanath was playing against the third generation of Indian bowlers, but there seemed to be zero effect of the newest lot on him. Left-arm paceman R.P. Singh in particular suffered a lot as he was taken for 26 off an over.

Sanath's efforts helped Sri Lanka win the Asia Cup, yet again. This knock came right after he had been dropped from the squad. The face-off against an Indian attack prolonged his career a little longer.

He had the fight for one more defining innings left in him—his last ODI century (107) against India in January 2009. This made him the oldest ODI centurion at 39, a record since broken by United Arab Emirates' Khurram Khan. But that final century against India did not yield a win. This summed up the shift in Sri Lanka's fortunes as India established a hold over them in all formats. It took a long time for India to shake off the after-effects of Sanath's brutal assault on an entire nation. Bruised egos of Indian cricketers in the late 1990s are a living testimony of his batting.

Everyone in India yearned for a Sanath prototype in the national team. The fans almost pleaded to replicate the Sanath model. It was best typified by the hoarding at a stadium in India during the 1996 World Cup—'Can't Indian mothers give birth to one Jayasuriya?'

4

Leading From the Front

Cricket in Sri Lanka was at an all-time high after the 1996 World Cup triumph. The members of that squad are still reaping the benefits of the win in some corners of Sri Lanka. The core group of that squad stuck together for a long time. But the first signs of a crack appeared when the mainstay of the side, Asanka Gurusinha, was sidelined in 1997. He quit cricket in a huff and moved to Australia. That was the first dent in a side that had appeared united, at least on the face of it.

As the 1999 ICC Cricket World Cup in England got closer, the pressure on Sri Lanka started mounting. More specifically, the pressure on the captain, Arjuna Ranatunga, and his deputy, Aravinda de Silva, was rising. There was a general perception that Sri Lanka could not mount a strong defence. The cry for fresh blood was still not strong enough.

Just a year before the World Cup, however, specifically in

January 1998, Sri Lanka, while playing Zimbabwe in a bilateral series, decided to experiment after a long time. Both Ranatunga and de Silva took a game off with the ODI series already sealed.

The job was handed to the much younger Sanath, and in his first game, he proved successful as a captain. Sri Lankan cricket had begun its succession planning without ever spelling it out openly. Then, in May 1998, when New Zealand was on tour, the selectors indicated Sanath's possible elevation to the top role in the future.

Sri Lanka huffed and puffed its way to the title defence in 1999 for the World Cup in England. There was a sense of expectation, but the side did not have the same aura that they had when they went all guns blazing in the 1996 World Cup. The side crashed out in grand style and did not even make it to the second stage of the tournament. There was a general sense of despondence and calls for making radical changes were getting louder.

As with most things in Sri Lankan cricket, political interference in this exit was also not too far off. Minister for Sports S.B. Dissanayake brought out the broom and dismissed the entire top brass of BCCSL. He put in place an interim committee to run the affairs, even as the World Cup was winding down. One key member of this interim committee, who was also named the new chairman of selectors, was former batsman Sidath Wettimuny. Wettimuny was a veteran of many years, having earned his stripes as a top-class batsman for Sri Lanka.

He began planning the next steps and put in place a plan to make a break from the past. One of the first steps he undertook was to make a trip to England to seek out an old Sri Lanka hand, Dav Whatmore. Whatmore was the coach who had been booted out in December 1996, just nine months after he had led the side to that famous World Cup win. Whatmore was now the coach of the English county side, Lancashire, and was based in Manchester. Wettimuny sought Whatmore out to see if he was keen to come back as the Sri Lanka head coach.

'Sidath was in London and wanted to come over to Manchester to talk to me. I still remember him coming over. He said we are making a change. We are going to get a young captain in and would like you to be with him,' Whatmore recalled to the author. 'He basically said we want you to begin from where you left off.'

Start of a New Era

But the name of the new captain was still not known. This was because, in the mind of Wettimuny, there was still an internal struggle about who it should be. De Silva was certainly not in the running, so it was between the two seniors, Hashan Tillakaratne and Roshan Mahanama.

Years later, Wettimuny spelt out the dilemma in his mind while talking to the Sri Lankan newspaper *The Island* about that moment:[41]

> Roshan was one of my favourites. I really liked him. If I were to be emotional, I would have picked Roshan. I was very fond of him and I felt he was a guy who played the game the way it had to be played. I felt Roshan was a role model. If I were to tell a youngster to follow a role model, that had to be Roshan. I would have gone for Roshan if I

[41]Rex Clementine, 'My First Preference for Captain was Roshan, Not Sanath', *The Island*, 12 February 2011.

had to take an emotional decision, but it's not a case of emotions. My emotions would have wanted to have either Roshan or maybe even Aravinda, who was a very dear friend of mine as captain.

But the selectors led by Wettimuny opted for Sanath and it was a tough ask for them.

If I remember right, why we opted for Sanath was Roshan was struggling for form at that point. We felt if he's struggling with form and if we brought him in at that stage, we are going to have a situation where he's going to struggle with captaincy as well as form. Then if he had struggled with captaincy, we wouldn't have had anyone to fall back on. We felt that our fall-back option would be poor. But we thought, if we go for someone else, let's say a performer like Sanath and if something happens, we had Roshan to fall back on. It was a very tough decision. All of us thought Roshan was the guy who had all the credentials. But he had this problem of form. He was struggling. I don't think we could have had the luxury of having a captain who was struggling with his form. I do feel really sorry that Roshan couldn't captain. He was my favourite. You have a favourite in the team and Roshan was my favourite. He was a lovely guy and I liked him really. But we had to make this hard decision.

Once the decision was made, Wettimuny picked up the phone and called Sanath at around 11 p.m., almost a week after he returned from England. The call was to inform Sanath about his appointment as the new captain of Sri Lanka.

Sanath's instant reaction was one of surprise. 'Frankly, I had no idea,' he said in an interview to ESPNcricinfo. 'I had returned from the 1999 World Cup in England without any runs (82 in five games). I was shocked.'[42]

Sanath was instantly worried about having to deal with the many seniors he had leapfrogged into pole position. 'There were many other senior players who could have easily been appointed ahead of me. But Wettimuny said the seniors would support me. The main reason given was they wanted to groom me for the future, and since I was playing well I was ready for the job.'[43]

At around the same time, Whatmore, also being chased by the England and Wales Cricket Board (ECB) to be their new coach, quit his role at Lancashire. Back in Sri Lanka, Ranatunga received a lot of criticism from Minister Dissanayake, forcing the former Sri Lankan captain to come out with an open letter, addressed to the 'cricket-loving public of Sri Lanka', in which Ranatunga vowed to continue playing. 'I wanted to express my profound regret to you all for the debacle of the Sri Lankan team. What I do wish to say is that it is my firm belief that I do have a few years of cricket left in me and if my services are wanted I am willing to represent my country in whatever capacity,' he said.[44]

But the selectors were keen to change the whole grammar of Sri Lankan cricket as they wanted to have two separate squads for the Tests and ODIs. As a result, both Ranatunga and de Silva were dropped from the ODIs for a tri-series against India and

---

[42]Interview by Nagraj Gollapudi, 'I'd Like to Play for Another Six Months', http://www.espncricinfo.com/magazine/content/story/441258.html, 27 December 2009.
[43]Ibid.
[44]'Ranatunga Asked to Step Down', https://www.rediff.com/worldcup99/srilanka/news/1206sri.htm, 12 June 1999.

Australia. But the veteran duo was retained for the Tests against Australia.

Wettimuny said, 'Having two separate squads will make a broader pool of resource available for selection. The idea behind selecting the one-day squad is in terms of long-term prospects, especially for the next World Cup.'[45]

South Africa-born former England captain Tony Greig, a long-term supporter of Sri Lankan cricket, was incensed with the decision to leave the veterans out. Greig 'confronted' Wettimuny over the decision.

'I convinced him (Greig) at the end of our conversation. He had nothing to say at the end. There are certain things that are confidential, but we made the decisions based on what we knew talking to the team,' Wettimuny told *The Island* in an interview.[46]

Sri Lanka had lost 18 of their 25 ODIs from October 1998 to May 1999. So a change was in the offing. 'There's a natural lethargy that sets in after you had won a World Cup. When the team had done so well, it is so natural that you lose your edge. You begin to slacken after you had done well,' he added.

The speculation over Whatmore's possible return ended as the former Australian batsman accepted the offer to become Sri Lanka's coach again. Sanath, however, was under no illusion that he had a tough task on hand. 'My biggest challenge was handling the senior players—Arjuna, Aravinda, Mahanama, Hashan.'

The first of that quartet to feel the brunt was Mahanama as

[45]'Ranatunga, de Silva Axed from One-day Team', https://www.rediff.com/sports/1999/aug/05axed.htm, 5 August 1999.
[46]Rex Clementine, 'My First Preference for Captain was Roshan, Not Sanath', *The Island*, 12 February 2011.

he left the game in a huff. 'If I couldn't be amongst the best 22 of the country, then I thought I should leave. I could have stayed on the board contract and kept getting money without playing. But I value my self-respect more than anything,' said Mahanama as he announced his immediate retirement from all forms of cricket.[47]

Another person who was sacked was long-term team manager and another former captain, Duleep Mendis, along with the coach, Roy Dias. Sri Lanka wanted to start off on a clean slate in a new era under a new leader. For the position of the manager, Mendis was replaced by former player Chandra Schafter. As the squad started preparing for the triangular series, one of the first acts of Sanath was to crack the whip, and it related not to any on-field issue, but an issue that is a major addiction now—use of mobile phones. In 1999, using a mobile phone was still a costly proposition and a fancy tool to have. It was neither smart nor useful in 1999, but it still managed to attract a lot of interest from everyone.

Naturally, the Sri Lankan cricketers were not to be left behind. Sri Lanka's squad had been gifted mobile phones by a private company before the World Cup in England in 1999. The entire squad was using mobile phones during the World Cup and it became a source of criticism as many felt that the players were distracted by the gifts. So, one of the first acts of Sanath as the captain, was to ban the use of mobile phones by players, even during practice. 'It is a big challenge. It is a big task,' he said in his first news conference after being appointed captain. 'I think

---

[47]'Hurt Mahanama Feels Sorry for Aravinda Too', *The Times of India*, 1 August 2001.

it is not proper to use cell phones even during practice and I am against it.'[48]

Later, just shortly before Sanath's first Test series as captain, Ranatunga was temporarily banned from attending practice sessions due to indiscipline. Ranatunga was penalized by the manager, Schafter, for not informing the BCCSL in writing before his departure to Canada where he played in a one-day exhibition match in Toronto, featuring Asian XI against World XI.

The controversy erupted after the veteran batsman's departure for Canada to play for Asian XI. Before leaving, Ranatunga said he had obtained permission from the Board's chairman, Rinsie Wijayathilaka, and Minister of Sports Dissanayake. But Ranatunga's trip proved futile as he was refused permission by the organizers there to play for Asian XI as he had not secured clearance from the Sri Lankan cricket board.

Schafter, who promised to enforce a strict code of discipline on the team, wrote to Ranatunga, seeking clarification on his sudden departure. 'Ranatunga was asked to submit a letter to the interim committee through me prior to his departure to Canada stating the reasons for his tour. But he went without following the procedure laid down by the board,' Schafter told *Daily News*.[49] This new Sri Lanka side meant business.

'Since my leaving (Sri Lanka) two and a half years, Sanath had become very much his own man. He had got to the stage where

[48]Kieran Daley. 'Cricket: Mendis Ousted as Sri Lankans Start Afresh', *Independent*, https://www.independent.co.uk/sport/cricket-mendis-ousted-as-sri-lankans-start-afresh-1106180.html, 13 July 1999.
[49]*The Tribune*, https://www.tribuneindia.com/1999/99aug13/sports.htm#7, 13 August 1999.

he was very much a definite contributor, but he was still not a senior,' Whatmore said in his first impression of the new captain. That certainly seemed to make an impact as Sri Lanka won the first two series with Sanath in charge. They first beat the much-fancied reigning world ODI champion, Australia, and India in the tri-series. Then, boosted by the arrival of Ranatunga, de Silva beat Australia for the first time in a Test series by 1-0. Any doubts Sanath had about the support he would get from the seniors were wiped out quite swiftly.

'They (seniors) always supported him. Once the game was to start, the training and preparation phase was to get into the right frame of mind and environment. Once you got to the ground, Sanath was the man. He was the sort of guy who welcomed leadership, because the extra responsibility helped him a lot. The older guys supported him a lot, because they played their hardest for the country. In team meetings, Arjuna was very good and Aravinda too backed the younger captain,' Whatmore recalled to the author.

Turning the Fortunes Around

Sri Lanka was on a roll thereafter, winning ODI and Test series in Zimbabwe and Pakistan. The side also won a number of ODI tri-series at home, in Sharjah and in New Zealand. It was Test cricket that needed improvement. Ranatunga called it a day in 2000, leaving a gaping hole in the Test XI. This is where the teamwork of Whatmore and Sanath came to the fore.

A number of young players were finding their feet and were keen to make a mark. Amongst them, Sanath's opening partner Marvan Atapattu was coming into his own.

'Marvi (Atapattu) was still very much a youngster. He did not have too many games behind him. He was a very good cricketer who was also keen to establish himself. He formed good combination with Sanath as openers. It was a good fit as he was as reserved and quiet as the captain,' Whatmore conveyed to the author.

Mahela Jayawardene was promoted to the role of Sanath's vice-captain. So Sanath had fresh ideas around him on the field. Whatmore had noted the improvement in Jayawardene since the time he had seen him as a teenager. Then there was another young player making his way to the top. This man, Kumar Sangakkara, would turn out to be the lynchpin of Sri Lankan cricket for the next decade and a half.

'We brought in Sanga (Sangakkara) in after a short A-team tour to South Africa. He came in and hit a very good 75 in Galle. He did a really good job. He was also a keeper. But unusually for a Sri Lankan batsman, [he was] quite at ease while playing pace,' said Whatmore to the author.

So the batting was finally taking some shape. Then there was the experience of de Silva who was still hungry to perform and was even brought back into the ODI XI to add experience.

Whatmore and Sanath then set about rebuilding the Test XI during which they lost to Pakistan, England (at home) and South Africa (away). But the floodgates finally opened with a series win over an injury-ridden Indian side led by Sourav Ganguly in August 2001.

Despite the injuries, Ganguly's team managed to level the series in Kandy and thereby brought the series to a mouthwatering climax in Colombo. Sanath was a worried man, because for the last two years, his side had rarely crossed the line in Test cricket. Things, however, changed with the side notching up a massive innings and

77 runs to finally win a Test series. Sanath was the happiest.

'We needed to start winning Test series and this victory will give the team a lot of confidence,' said a relieved Sanath. The lack of wins in Test cricket was showing on him too.

'We have not won a series since we beat Pakistan last year and this was a crucial win.'[50]

Batting finally came good, proving to be a huge relief to Sanath. 'We have been let down by the batsmen in the past few series, but they came back well in this game to score 600 runs,' he said. 'We had a meeting with all the batsmen after the Kandy Test where I told them to play their natural game, but to make sure they get the big scores once they are well set.'[51]

Everything seemed to be finally falling in place in Test cricket. Champion spinner Muttiah Muralitharan had a lot of support, apart from the left-arm paceman Chaminda Vaas. There was a young fast bowler Dilhara Fernando who bowled with a lot of pace. The experienced Tillakaratne, too, made a return after two years. So, the side finally had a strong nucleus to work with.

But just around this time, there was another storm waiting to hit Sri Lankan cricket, and more specifically, Sanath. His long-term teammate and close friend, Mahanama, had just penned down his autobiography, *Retired Hurt*. In the book, Mahanama alleged that Australian paceman Glenn McGrath had racially abused Sanath, calling him 'black monkey'.

The incident, alleged Mahanama, happened on the 1995–96 tour to Australia during the second final of the annual tri-series

---

[50]Charlie Austen, Sri Lanka Seal Silent Victory in Colombo', ESPNcricinfo, 2 September 2001.
[51]Ibid.

played down under. The book was released in Australia and created a lot of furore. McGrath denied the claim and even threatened legal action. Aussies claimed that Mahanama was not playing the game so he could not write what he had written. But Mahanama stuck to his guns.

India, New Zealand and the Sri Lankan squad, including Sanath, attended the launch as they were all in town for a tri-series. In the presence of the entire cricket fraternity, including commentators, members of parliament, ex-cricketers and diplomats, Mahanama played some clips from the match to prove his point. The clip showed McGrath standing in Sanath's way while the batsman was looking for a run. The video footage also showed McGrath using foul language at the Sri Lankan opener. The video exhibited Umpire Steve Randell pointing out the incident to the then Australian captain Mark Taylor. But these distractions did little to spoil Sanath's frame of mind. He was settling down into his role, two years after he first took over.

'He was a popular guy in the team. The best thing about him was that he never stopped having a laugh. He would joke in Sinhalese with the team. My communication with him was good, even though he did not speak that great English. But I had a sense of the humour that he had. He always saw the funny side of things,' said Whatmore to the author.

That sort of rubbed off on the rest of the side as Sri Lanka won eight Tests in a row post the India series win. This also included a 3-0 win against West Indies at home where a rampaging Brian Lara smashed 513 runs. The final win in this glorious run ended with a title win in the Asian Test Championship, played without India, in Lahore.

First Signs of Trouble

Around twelve months before the World Cup in 2003, Sri Lanka finally seemed to be setting their house in order. Their ODI squad was in a good space and the Test squad, too, had found its bearings.

With such a record behind them, Sanath led his side to what turned out to be the most defining phase of his captaincy. This phase in the lead up to the World Cup, was to define his legacy as a captain. The first stop in this journey was England, as it was the third-ranked Test side. Sri Lanka's winning run in Tests ended here, and for the first time, Sanath, too, faced a lot of criticism from his critics, who had been waiting anxiously for him to slip.

Sri Lanka lost the Test series by 0-2, leading to a spate of criticism. There were also rumours of a dressing room spat. In particular, the questions were raised around Sanath's decision-making abilities. Muralitharan played a Test despite not being fully fit after a shoulder surgery.

Then, Sanath dropped himself down the order for the third Test, making Russel Arnold open the batting. All these decisions led to sharp words from Sanath's former captain, Ranatunga.

'It is a decision made without consideration for the way that it will be received by the opposition,' Ranatunga wrote in his Sunday newspaper column.[52]

'Sanath may feel he is not batting well and that is understandable, but to protect himself and to throw into the openers slot Russel Arnold, in very difficult conditions, beggars belief. Most significantly, the message it sends to the opposition is that the captain doesn't

---

[52]Martin Gough, 'Captaincy in Question', http://news.bbc.co.uk/sport2/hi/cricket/england/2051534.stm, 18 June 2002.

fancy it. And if he isn't up for the fight, what about his team?'[53]

Former chief selector Wettimuny, who had thrust Sanath into the leader's role three years ago, also joined in, 'They have been on a high through the last nine Tests and suddenly they're on the defensive. They seem to have lost confidence and that has shown in their body language. Some of these guys need talking to all the time. They fall short in confidence and this is something we have seen for a long time in our cricket.'[54]

There was usual chaos in the administration along with political interference within the BCCSL. So, for the first time in three years, there seemed to be pressure on Sanath. It surely was a test.

Sanath was also involved in a battle of attrition with the selection panel. First in January 2002, the selectors wanted to 'rest' Atapattu for a Test against touring Zimbabwe at Kandy. Sanath directly reached out to the Minister of Sports, Johnston Fernando, who got the decision reversed and the entire selection panel was booted out.

Then, in July of the same year, a new set of selectors led by the no-nonsense wicketkeeper-batsman Guy de Alwis tried something similar against touring Bangladesh. In the second and final Test of that tour, de Alwis' panel rested six of the seniors, angering Sanath further.

'I do not agree with the resting of six seniors, especially Muralitharan... Having said that, I have to go with the team the selectors give and that is what I will do in the second Test,' fumed Sanath.[55]

---

[53]Ibid.

[54]Ibid.

[55]Roshan Abeysinghe, 'Sri Lanka at loggerheads', http://www.island. lk/2002/08/04/sports12.html.

As if to prove Sanath right, Sri Lanka struggled on the opening day of the Test at Colombo's Sinhalese Sports Club leading to further frustration. 'They showed us today that they cannot be taken lightly,' said a frustrated Sanath at the end of the first day's play. This was later recounted to the author.

Minister for Sports, Fernando, did call for an emergency meeting with de Alwis, Whatmore and Sanath to resolve this issue. But de Alwis refused to budge. With a crucial ICC Champions Trophy set to be staged at home, the focus of the final stretch before the World Cup switched completely to ODI cricket. But before that, there was a major battle to be fought with the Sri Lankan players led by Sanath refusing to play the tournament, owing to a contentious ambush marketing clause.

Most of the world's leading players, especially from Australia, England, India and South Africa, had objected to the presence of a clause in ICC's contracts for major events, which barred them from having personal sponsorship deals competing with their own. This proved to be a major sticking point. Australian, English, and South African players came around after protracted discussions. India, on the other hand, had players who stood their ground. Similar issues engulfed Sri Lanka, too, with the players refusing to play the tournament.

A Sri Lankan Cricketers' Association (SLCA) was formed in 1999–2000 thanks to the efforts of Mahanama. Former fast bowler Graeme Labrooy, too, joined in, playing a crucial role in conveying the demands of the players to BCCSL.

Sri Lanka's cricketers had two demands:

a) The players wanted a 30 per cent share of the money that the ICC paid the BCCSL for ICC events.

b) The players demanded that ICC consult them before they
    agree to match sponsorship deals.

Sri Lankan players were willing to compromise if the ICC met
them halfway. 'We don't see any real danger for the tournament.
The game must go on and we feel there will be give and take on
both sides,' said Labrooy to the author. The former fast bowler said
the players were being provided legal advice to ensure that there
was no conflict of interest. 'We feel that there should be greater
dialogue between the players and the ICC in deciding their course
of action for the next three to four years,' Labrooy said. 'That way,
we should be able to avoid this type of situation.'

BCCSL and SLCA reached a compromise just twelve days
before the start of the tournament. An agreement was reached
after the BCCSL promised to pay the players an 'undisclosed lump
sum' as compensation for the use of their player rights. Although
the players failed to get the 30 per cent share from ICC revenue,
Labrooy was satisfied with the final outcome. Even though that
was a solution, the threat of a possible future lockdown always
remained.

Sri Lanka, meanwhile, continued to build very nicely for the
Champions Trophy, besting South Africa and Pakistan in a tri-
nation tournament played for the first time in Morocco. The hero
of the triumph was the captain himself who had got into a rich
vein of form as the highest run-getter for the tournament with
299 runs from five games. Leading into the Champions Trophy,
however, there was an injury scare as he dislocated his shoulder in
Morocco. But he recovered in time for the ICC event. His good
form continued with a string of scores that led Sri Lanka to the
finals against India. Since the start of the Morocco Cup, they had

the following string of scores—36, 102 not out, 71, 46, 97, 49, 36, 42 and 74.

Unfortunately, rain played spoilsport not once but twice, in two days in the finals, leaving the two teams to share the trophy and the spoils. This was also the last time Aravinda de Silva was to play on Sri Lankan soil and he was given a hearty farewell. But then, the ugly dispute with the selection panel raised its head. Minister Fernando refused to ratify the squad that was chosen to tour South Africa after a direct personal plea from Sanath to include the uncapped twenty-year fast-bowling all-rounder Kaushalya Weeraratne.

De Alwis' panel, in consultation with Sanath, Whatmore and strategic consultant Duleep Mendis, had picked the 16-man squad for the South Africa Test tour. Minister Fernando sent a letter to de Alwis, asking his panel to 'reconsider' their selection. De Alwis categorically refused to make any changes.

'We will not change the 16 that we have picked,' confirmed de Alwis to ESPNcricinfo. 'It could kill youngsters to drop them now. We will have to see if a compromise can be reached but all the 16 are going to South Africa.'[56]

De Alwis also reacted angrily to suggestions that Sanath had not been properly consulted. 'Next time we have a selection committee meeting I will be taking a video camera so that no one can say he was not properly consulted—Sanath Jayasuriya was at the meeting.'[57]

Finally, as a compromise, instead of Weeraratne, left-arm

[56]Charlie Austen, 'Sri Lanka in Selection Chaos Over South Africa Tour Squad', ESPNcricinfo, 10 October 2002.
[57]Ibid.

paceman Ruchira Perera was drafted in as an additional seventeenth member of the squad.

Despite all these problems, the progress made by Sanath's side was seen not in terms of results, but in terms of approach, especially on the tough tour of South Africa. Despite the losses in the ODI and Test series, even hard-nosed critics like former South African spinner Pat Symcox praised the side in his syndicated column for ESPNcricinfo.[58]

> Sri Lankan Test cricket took a giant leap forward in the second Test against South Africa at Supersport Park. It was a match that will long be remembered for its intensity and evenness, but sadly, it will also be remembered for the wrong reasons.
>
> The sledging that went on was not acceptable in the Test arena. Who started it and who was the guiltiest will never be proved conclusively but one thing is for sure, both sides never took a backward step. It is for this very reason that I believe that Sri Lankan cricket took a huge step forward.
>
> History will record a 2-0 win to South Africa, but from now on, the knowledge that they can compete if they stand tall and take up the challenge without flinching, will ensure that the present players are competitive even in the face of adversity. This is the way that the Australians and South Africans learn to play. It is an integral part of the game at most levels and it has a way of separating the men from the boys very quickly.

---

[58]Pat Symcox, 'Sri Lanka Test Cricket Takes a Giant Leap', ESPNcricinfo, 22 November 2002.

But even in those moments of high, the issue of the ICC player contracts cropped up again. Left hanging in September 2002, the problem surfaced in the new year, just before the World Cup in South Africa. This time, there were a group of five Sri Lankan players who were refusing to sign the player contracts citing the contentious ICC marketing clause. Sanath was one of the five, and in a way, he had become a symbol of the resistance.

Sri Lanka was touring Australia for a tri-series also featuring England. Labrooy began a peace mission to Australia and persuaded the players to sign the contract 'for the greater good'. But Sanath's stance invited a lot of criticism, especially from the media. The Upali group of newspapers went hammer and tongs at Sanath. The group's two newspapers—*The Island* (English) and *Divaina* (in Sinhala)—were critical of Sanath's decision.

'None of the Sri Lankan players had contracts with rival products of the tournament sponsors and they were just asking for more money. That was the reason for our brutal attack even calling for his sacking,' wrote *The Island*'s cricket writer Rex Clementine, a few years later, about that incident.[59]

Finally, Sanath did come around, but daggers were drawn.

Final Stretch

Just before the World Cup, Sanath successfully resisted the selectors' decision to leave out Jayawardene, but had to settle for left-hand batsman Jehan Mubarak in the squad. When Sri Lanka began its 2003 World Cup campaign, Sanath had more battles to

---

[59]Rex Clementine, 'The Legend Who Makes Us Look Stupid', *The Island*, 27 June 2011.

fight. Sanath had a greater duty of protecting his players, especially his star spinner, Muralitharan. Yet again, Murali had come under fire from experts, who questioned his bowling action. Former New Zealand cricketer Ian Smith wrote a book released just in time for Sri Lanka's opening game against New Zealand, where he called him a 'chucker' and said that the off-spinner broke the game's rules.

Sanath stoutly defended the spinner. 'He (Murali) wants to win the World Cup, so do we, and it is affecting him. He's taken a few things personally and it's hard not to. He realizes he's in the public eye and he's big news all the time, but sometimes you can destroy him if you go too far.'[60]

Next up, Sanath tackled his critics with his match-winning knock of 120, his first in a World Cup, against New Zealand. It was clear that he was sending a strong message. 'In Sri Lanka's first ever game in that World Cup at Bloemfontein against New Zealand he scored a brilliant hundred and at the media conference, gave us that cheeky smile, driving home the point,' recalled Clementine.[61]

Then, Sri Lanka was doing well, thrashing Bangladesh by 10 wickets. In this contest, Chaminda Vaas created a record by claiming a hat-trick off the first three balls of the match.

In the next game against Canada, Sri Lanka handed out a masterclass as they bowled out their rivals for the lowest-ever ODI score of 36. It seemed that Sri Lanka would continue doing well, but they hit an unexpected roadblock. In a shocking result,

---

[60]'Jayasuriya Fearful for Murali', http://news.bbc.co.uk/sport3/cwc2003/hi/newsid_2740000/newsid_2741800/2741859.stm, 10 February 2003.
[61]Rex Clementine, 'The Legend Who Makes Us Look Stupid', *The Island*, 27 June 2011.

Sri Lanka crashed to a 53-run defeat at the hands of Kenya. Both Sanath and Whatmore were fuming at the result.

'I think it's one of the worst matches I've ever played; 211 is an attainable total but that was disappointing. We did not play like professionals today, we played like amateurs. We batted badly and our middle order didn't click. This is my and the team's worst day in cricket,' thundered Sanath in Nairobi post the loss.[62]

In Whatmore's view, the batting was an issue, though they still managed to pull things back, first against West Indies and then against South Africa in the final league match, which was to decide their passage to the Super Six stage. This match at Durban proved to be memorable in many ways as South Africa famously self-destructed and forgot the rules that governed a rain-affected match. South Africa needed just a single to go past the par score, but instead, their keeper-batsman Mark Boucher chose to pat the ball down as the match ended in a tie. South Africa was booted out from their own World Cup. Sri Lanka got through, owing to a superior run-rate, leading to contrasting moments from both camps. South African captain Shaun Pollock was later sacked from his job but Sri Lanka kept afloat.

In the second phase, Sri Lanka began with a heavy loss to Australia, which also led to Sanath's thumb being fractured and left arm bruised. Despite not being fit, Sanath took a risk and played in the deflating 183-run defeat at the hands of India, which completely derailed the campaign. Sri Lanka had crumbled to 109 all out—their second lowest World Cup score ever.

---

[62]"Furious Jayasuriya Brands Performance "Amateurish", ESPNcricinfo, http://www.espncricinfo.com/ci/content/story/126945.html, 25 February 2003.

Sanath received a lot of criticism from former cricketers for asking India to bat first on a track that was seemingly tailor-made for batsmen. But he strongly defended his decision.

'We did not bowl well and did not bat well either. It was a very disappointing game for us,' said Sanath after the defeat. 'I think I was right to ask India to bat in the morning because there was bounce in the wicket, but except for Chaminda Vaas none of the bowlers did their job.'[63]

Due to a variety of results in other matches, Sri Lanka still had a chance to make it to the semi-finals. Finally, when they beat Zimbabwe by 74 runs, their spot was sealed. They were to play the rampaging Australia side at Port Elizabeth. The result of that day in Port Elizabeth still hurts Whatmore. In a low-scoring match, made more famous by Adam Gilchrist's famous sporting walk, Sri Lanka struggled throughout. The dream of making to the finals for the first time since 1996 came crashing down.

'We were pretty confident of upsetting a strong Australian team. But there were a few different things that happened that day. First, Sanga dropped Symonds. Then we just could not keep going while chasing 220 (212-7). Aravinda (de Silva) got run out. It was never easy; everyone was down. I still remember everyone going quiet,' recalled Whatmore to the author.

The exit meant that de Silva had ended his career abruptly. Sanath was a broken man after the loss as he was yet again let down by the batting lineup. 'The key was not to lose wickets in the first 10 to 15 overs. This was the kind of pitch we were used

---

[63]'Jayasuriya Defends Toss Decision', http://news.bbc.co.uk/sport3/cwc2003/hi/newsid_2830000/newsid_2837100/2837173.stm, 10 March 2003.

to. The bowlers bowled well and we fielded well,' he lamented in the post-match conference.[64]

Whatmore knew his days were numbered and was aware Sanath wanted out. The pre-tournament media scrum against Sanath was the clearest indication that he was going to step down. 'I am sure he would have had some pressures from different areas, media not being the least. But still I thought that reaching the semi-final of a World Cup was a good effort. Looking back, we were one win away from playing the final,' added Whatmore.

As expected, after the exit from the World Cup, Sanath handed his resignation to Minister Fernando. 'I have tendered my resignation to the minister of sports,' he was quoted as saying. 'With my decision I have given the selectors the chance to opt for a new captain with the 2007 World Cup in mind.'[65]

But the minister refused to accept the resignation. 'I appreciate Sanath's freedom to send in his resignation. The authorities also have the freedom to reject or accept it.'[66]

Sanath wanted Whatmore to continue, though he had put himself on notice. 'Dav has been doing a good job and he has been very good for the boys,' said Sanath. 'He has been there for a long time and when he has been there we have achieved a lot of things.'[67]

One of Sanath's *bête noires* during this final phase of his captaincy, de Alwis, too stepped down as chief selector, citing

---

[64]Ibid.

[65]'Jayasuriya Keen to Quit', http://news.bbc.co.uk/sport3/cwc2003/hi/newsid_2870000/newsid_2876100/2876195.stm, 23 March 2003.

[66]Charlie Austin, 'Sanath Jayasuriya Offers his Resignation', ESPNcricinfo, , 23 March 2003.

[67]'Sri Lanka Coach Whatmore Set for Talks Over Future', http://www.island.lk/2003/03/21/sports02.html

government interference. Sanath was told to stay on as he took his charges to Sharjah for a four-nation tournament, but Whatmore left as expected. However, Sanath reiterated his stand to quit. BCCSL Chief Executive Anura Tennekoon gave a strong indication of Sanath's mindset.

'He has indicated that he would like to relinquish the captaincy but he has not officially informed us yet. On his return from Sharjah he is likely to indicate what his position is,' said Tennekoon.[68] On his part, Sanath told the broadcaster Ten Sports in Sharjah that the time had come for a new leader.

'I was asked to continue for Sharjah but after this they will have to find someone else to do the job,' said Sanath. 'I have made my decision and I will continue as a player.' Explaining his decision further, he said, 'After the World Cup I thought the time had come to groom someone for the 2007 World Cup.'[69]

Finally, a week after the early exit from the Sharjah Cup, Sanath officially tendered his resignation again. Chief selector Lalith Kaluperuma confirmed receiving Sanath's resignation and said that he had begun looking for alternatives. Sanath had nominated his long-term vice-captain, Atapattu, as his successor. 'It is for them (selectors) to find a replacement. But my personal thinking is that Marvan should take over—he has a lot of experience and has been vice-captain for some time now.'

The selectors took Sanath's suggestion on board, but split the role between Atapattu for ODIs and Tillakaratne for the Tests as Sri Lanka entered a period of uncertainty.

---

[68]'Sanath Jayasuriya to Resign from Captaincy after Sharjah Cup', rediff.com, 9 April 2003.
[69]Ibid.

5
—

Just Another Player

Sometimes in cricket, when you quit captaincy and go back to the ranks, it can get a bit awkward at times. A former captain and a current captain in the same setup is not the ideal situation in squads.

Former England Captain Nasser Hussain in his autobiography, *Playing with Fire,* wrote about how the dynamics within the team changed quickly after he quit the leadership role. In particular, he narrated incidents with certain senior players, who had conveyed to him quite clearly that there was no need for him to worry.

Another former captain, Ricky Ponting, of Australia, spent a decade in the role, winning two World Cups. But when he quit his role, he very swiftly dropped down the food chain. There were, in fact, concerns within the Australian setup on how the former and current captain (Michael Clarke) would work together.

Ponting then was at pains to explain to people that he would never come in anyone's way. 'I'll help Pup (Clarke) out as much as I can. But only if I'm asked. If I'm not asked, I'll sit back and prepare and play like an everyday player.'

In his autobiography, *Ponting at the Close of Play*, Ponting writes about an embarrassing moment in the first tour post captaincy. He was not told that he was not required for a team think-tank session, but he assumed he was. He knocked on the door to find the captain, vice-captain, coach and manager. The quartet had to sheepishly inform Ponting that he was not required there.

Something similar was in store for Sanath in his time post captaincy as he very quickly slipped down the ranks. After four years in charge, in probably the most successful phase in Sri Lankan cricket, Sanath found the setup very chaotic.

Sri Lanka started off with two separate captains in Hashan Tillakaratne (Tests) and Marvan Atapattu (ODIs) for the first twelve months after Sanath stepped down. The changeover, at least in the ODIs, appeared seamless. It was in the Tests that the problem first cropped up.

But Sanath had problems of his own. Runs were not coming at the same clip as before and the big centuries were no longer the order of the day. With him stepping down, the scrutiny about his place in the playing XI started getting denser by the day.

He had only four half-centuries as 'just a player' in ten Test matches till Australia under first-time captain Ponting came calling in March 2004. This was when Sanath finally came into the fore. He had endured a forgettable ODI series, but in the Tests that followed, pressure on Sanath was increasing.

In the second innings of the second Test of the series, Sanath was back at his devastating best. At the Asgiriya Stadium in Murali's hometown of Kandy, both sides were involved in a low-scoring slugfest. Set to chase a stiff 352 to level the series, Sanath set off in his trademark style, smashing 131 off just 145 balls with 17 hits to the fence and 2 sixes. But that was not enough as Sri Lanka lost not just the Test by 27 runs, but also the series. It was a complete whitewash in the end as Australia romped home by 3-0 in the series. Tillakaratne lost his job and the Test squad of Sri Lanka endured another round of uncertainty.

Meanwhile, in ODIs, Sanath had gone 31 ODIs without a century until the Asia Cup came calling at home in 2004. There was talk about the diminishing returns from one-time marauder in the shorter versions.

Already thirty-five, the talk about trying out a younger lot started, with a view of building towards the 2007 World Cup in West Indies. Sanath's lean patch had stretched for close to seventeen months. But the captain, Atapattu, stood by him. 'He is invaluable, has the ability to turn a match on its head in any of the three departments of the game. I'm waiting for that one good innings. After that he'll be the Jayasuriya we know,' said Atapattu.[70]

And it came!

Not one, but two back-to-back centuries against Bangladesh, and then, against his favourite side, India. Sanath was all praises for his skipper's support. 'Marvan was absolutely wonderful. Every time someone took my name, he'd say, "I have full faith in Sanath. I know his ability."'[71]

It was a-run-a-ball 107 against Bangladesh, but the knock (132-ball 130) against India was worth noting because of his stroke play (13 boundaries and a six).

[70]Sanjay Rajan, The Lion's on The Prowl Again', *The Hindu*, 29 July 2004.
[71]Ibid.

'I feel happy to have scored consecutive centuries. I'm also thrilled to have come off a lean patch. A comeback of sorts,' Sanath said.[72] It was a knock in vain as India managed to pull off a win, but Sanath was nevertheless happy to prove his critics wrong.

'I understand their (critics) point. I hadn't got a one-day century in a long time. It was something that I had to accept. In fact, it egged me on. Have to thank them for it.'[73]

With his ODI reputation restored, Sanath still had to justify his place in the Test squad. A tour to Pakistan that followed did the job of ensuring that Sanath's place was assured for some time to come. In the first Test at Faisalabad, Sanath played a knock that typified his nature with the bat. He struck the third and last double century (253) of his Test career to set up a famous win for his side. The highlight of this knock was a 101-run stand for the ninth wicket with tail-ender Dilhara Fernando, who contributed a grand total of 1!

'I have never thought about individual landmarks,' he said, 'but getting such a score obviously is very pleasing. It is always important for me when I get runs outside Sri Lanka but I am satisfied today because I scored runs when my team needed it the most.'

Pakistan's coach, the late Bob Woolmer, hoped his side would get inspired to play after watching Sanath play. 'We are looking for players to bat for two days in Test matches just like Jayasuriya did,' said Woolmer. Pakistan did learn as they managed to square the two Test series, but not before Sanath slammed a second century (107) in the series at Karachi. This century at Karachi was also incidentally Sanath's last in his Test career, which also fetched him a Player of the Series award. This capped an unforgettable year for

[72]Ibid.
[73]Ibid.

Sanath in Test matches, his best since the salad days of 1997. In all, Sanath scored 1130 runs from 11 Tests with 4 centuries in the calendar year of 2004, at an average of 56.50. He was at an all-time high and was perhaps in a mood to celebrate.

But nature had something else in mind. In the early hours of 26 December 2004 when most regions in the world were asleep, a calamity struck. The Indian Ocean experienced a tsunami that devastated South East Asia, Sri Lanka and eastern coast of India. Around 230,000 people were reportedly dead in the tsunami, including 30,000 in Sri Lanka. Sanath experienced a personal tragedy in this catastrophe as his beloved town of Matara too was struck by the fury of the waves. In fact, when the waves hit the coast, Sanath was playing an ODI in Auckland against New Zealand. The tour was immediately abandoned as many players were affected personally by the tragedy.

'I could not get through to Sri Lanka because the communication lines were so bad,' Sanath said. Later it was revealed that his mother (Breeda) too was caught in the melee. 'I later found out that somebody had rescued my mother. She is recovering.'

The story goes that it was Sanath's name that helped his mother (Breeda Jayasuriya) survive the tsunami. She was swept away by the first wave and only by calling out to get attention, by saying that she was Sanath's mother, did a rescuer spot her among the debris and pull her to safety. But thousands of others, some Sanath's friends, were not so lucky. 'Even now when many people hear the word (tsunami), they are still scared. When my mother hears it, she still can't run,' Sanath recalled a few years later in an interview to CNN.[74]

---

[74]'Sanath Jayasuriya: Sri Lanka's Humble Cricketing Hero', http://edition.cnn.com/2008/WORLD/asiapcf/12/09/ta.jayasuriya/, 17 December 2008.

Leg-spinner Upul Chandana's mother was caught in the waves but survived, but fast bowlers Nuwan Zoysa's and Dilhara Fernando's relatives were not so lucky. Later, as Sanath was preparing for a tsunami charity match in Melbourne, he heard that the bodies of his friends were being recovered and identified.

Sanath had to pick up the pieces of his life post this tragedy, and he did just that with a stint at the English county side, Somerset, in the summer of 2005. Sanath was standing in for Ponting who was leading Australia for the now famous Ashes series. In fact, not many realize that it was Sanath and then South African skipper Graeme Smith who dented Australia early on during that tour.

In a one-day tour game before the series began, both Sanath and Smith pummeled Australia into submission. Set to chase an imposing 342 for 5, Sanath (101) and Smith (108) added 197 for the opening wicket in 22.3 overs. Somerset won the contest by 4 wickets and planted the first seed of doubt in the Aussie minds.

Signs of Insecurity

But back home, the message had obviously not been clear enough. He faced the first taste of pressure after the tremendous year of 2004. There was a change of guard with a new coach, Tom Moody. Atapattu, Sanath's support, was also under a lot of pressure following a series of injuries. Sanath was dropped from the Test squad for the series in India in late 2005. Accusations flew thick and fast on how this had happened.

Lalith Kaluperuma, the chairman of selectors, said in a SLC media release that Sanath was dropped after consulting Atapattu and Moody. But the *Daily News* reported that Atapattu denied being consulted in this regard.

On their part, the selectors pinned the blame on the team management for Sanath's axe. In a tersely worded media release, the selectors denied all accusations:

The National Coach Mr Tom Moody whilst in the process of team building prior to the departure of the Sri Lanka National team to India arranged a trip down South coast to participate in a Water Sports event. Sanath whilst participating in the said event met with an accident attributing to a shoulder injury which was not brought to the notice of the panel of selectors or SLC management at any stage.

Sanath, despite the injury, did proceed with the Sri Lanka National team to India to participate in the One-Day Series.

The tour selectors on tour, despite his injury did select him to play in the first ODI match and his body movement whilst bowling and fielding made it evident that his performance was below par.

Sanath's performance throughout the tour during the ODI Series either in batting, bowling or fielding was not upto expected standard, obviously owing to his shoulder injury. The panel of national selectors therefore decided to keep him out of the Indian Test Series so that he could obtain proper medical treatment and recover from the injury to be considered for the New Zealand Tour.

Sanath was determined to fight back. 'I was feeling disappointed on the day the team left for India,' he said. 'This setback has made me more determined and increased my hunger for runs. I had some injuries and then form too deserted me but I am keen to work hard on my game and get back in the team.'

'It's actually a bit difficult to cope with it when you are out of the side but it's a part of the game when you are a professional and I am cool about it,' he added.[75]

And he did fight back. Sanath made a return to the squad for the tour to New Zealand over the course of Christmas and New Year of 2006. This return was prompted mainly because of a wave of protest throughout Sri Lanka and biting media criticism. To make the whole process interesting, Sri Lanka's new president Mahinda Rajapakse, too, ordered a government probe into the axing of Sanath. With this in the background, a Sanath recall was an easy pick.

But fate had something else in store, yet again. Sanath's New Zealand tour ended abruptly as he dislocated his shoulder in the bathroom. 'Sanath was reaching for his shampoo when he slipped and fell in his bath,' Michael Tissera, the then Sri Lanka team manager said.

The bad spell of injuries continued with a thigh strain forcing him to miss more matches, this time at home against Pakistan in an ODI series. But he was back in the side for the Test series in March 2006. However, after making only 6 and 13 in the first Test, he handed his letter of retirement to SLC Chief Executive Duleep Mendis.

Sanath, then thirty-six, said, 'I thought about it long and hard and decided that is it. It's a very emotional moment.' But he was keen to prolong his ODI career so as to play in the upcoming ICC Cricket World Cup in March–April 2007. The then chairman of selectors Lalith Kaluperuma welcomed the move. 'I think that the decision to retire from Tests and the decision to play one-day cricket only is a very important one for Sri Lanka,' Kaluperuma

---

[75]'Jayasuriya Vows to Return', ESPNcricinfo, http://www.espncricinfo.com/srilanka/content/story/227461.html, 28 November 2005.

said. 'I know it is a huge vacuum to fill and it will never be easy to do so, but we will have to move on. We are confident that Sanath's decision will help him and Sri Lanka cricket tremendously, especially with the World Cup in 2007.'[76]

Jayawardene, then his junior teammate, paid rich tributes to his senior pro. 'Sanath's contribution to cricket in Sri Lanka has been immense. His brilliant statistics tell only half the story—he has been a match-winner on so many occasions with both bat and ball.'

Unfortunately, Sanath's Test career ended in misery, with another injury. In what was to be his final Test, against Pakistan at Kandy, he split his webbing while attempting a catch off opener Imran Farhat at gully.

'It looks like he will be out for at least four weeks. There's also a dislocation near the joint. It is unlikely that he will take any further part in the Test,' Tommy Simsek, Sri Lankan team's physiotherapist, told reporters at the Kandy Central Hospital.

But if you think there were no more twists and turns, then you are wrong.

Back with a Bang

Sri Lanka was touring England under new captain, Jayawardene, with Atapattu being forced out due to a back injury. As with most things in Sri Lankan cricket, politics brought about an unexpected change. Kaluperuma was out as chief selector and former fast bowler Asantha de Mel made a return in his place just a year after he had himself been booted out. In the musical chairs that is

---

[76]'Jayasuriya Set to End Test Career', http://news.bbc.co.uk/sport2/hi/cricket/4865492.stm, 31 March 2006.

Sri Lankan cricket, this was par for the course. But what followed was certainly not. In his first interview after taking over the role, de Mel blamed the SLC Interim Committee for the 'mess' as the side had slipped from number two to six in ODI rankings and from four to seven in Test Matches. Then he dropped a bombshell in another interview to *The Sunday Island*, where he claimed that Sanath had been forced to retire from Test cricket. De Mel claimed that the decision to retire hadn't come from Sanath and he had been forced to do so by Kaluperuma. De Mel said:

> I have very reliable information that he was forced to retire. I was surprised when I heard that he was going to retire. If a player wants to retire he does that before a series, but on this instance (sic) he was forced to retire and for me it's totally wrong. They should have at least respected the man because he has done so much for the country, but on this instance he was basically asked to pack his bags and go home. I can tell you that he's undoubtedly the fittest in the team and if you take the current crop of players and ask them to do a 100-metre sprint he will come first. When the selectors knew that Marvan is not going to make it to England with his back problem they should have continued with Jayasuriya. He just played a county season in England last year and knows the conditions well and is the only Sri Lankan to have scored a double hundred in England. What more credentials do you want?'[77]

The Sunday Island claimed to have carried out its own investigation and 'confirmed' de Mel's claim about the hand.

---

[77]'Jayasuriya Was Forced to Retire from Tests—de Mel', ESPNcricinfo, http://www.espncricinfo.com/srilanka/content/story/246407.html, 7 May 2006.

'Sri Lanka now has two inexperienced openers in Upul Tharanga and Michael Vandort and any bowling attack would love to bowl at them instead of Jayasuriya, even when he is out of form. All I can say is that the selectors got their onions mixed up,' de Mel added.[78]

Then came the big surprise. De Mel announced that he could persuade Sanath to possibly come out of retirement. In England, the Sri Lankan think-tank was dismayed with these comments. Coach Moody was also at the heart of de Mel's verbal attacks. 'I wonder whether Tom is the right candidate. He's basically a coach who speaks of strategy. If we take John Dyson (former coach) he was very professional. As chairman of selectors I had a lot of arguments and disagreements with him but he provided the results. You've got to face the fact that during John's time we were number two in the world,' de Mel said.[79]

All these comments in the lead-up to the first Test against England did not help the buildup. Moody was reported to have telephoned a top official of SLC to complain about de Mel. But Moody denied everything. 'I've lodged nothing,' Moody told AFP at Lord's. 'I've heard what you heard, a quote about the retirement of Sanath Jayasuriya. As far as we're concerned, I had a conversation with the chairman of selectors this morning and it didn't even come into the conversation.'[80]

Sanath, however, made a dramatic comeback from Test

---

[78] Rex Clementine, Sanath Was Forced to Retire', http://www.island.lk/2006/05/07/sports1.html

[79] 'Moody Denies Lodging Complaint', ESPNcricinfo, http://www.espncricinfo.com/engvsl/content/story/246581.html, 9 May 2006.

[80] 'Modi Denies Lodging Complaint', Cricinfo, http://www.espncricinfo.com/engvsl/content/story/246581.html, 9 May 2006.

retirement. He was added to the Test squad just after the first Test. But Moody and the new captain, Jayawardene, backed the new openers despite de Mel's outburst. Despite this, after a loss in the second Test, Sanath was named in the playing team XI for the decider at Trent Bridge.

'If we have Sanath it gives us more depth and experience, as well as another bowling option,' Jayawardene explained to BBC Sport.[81]

Even though Sanath made a dramatic return to Test cricket, he did not score more than 4 in each innings. He did not open either, as he batted down the order. But he did pick up 3 wickets as Sri Lanka won the Test by 134 runs to level the three-match series by 1–1.

Then, Sri Lanka got into the act of making it the most English summer as they hammered the hosts in all five ODIs that followed and the one-off Twenty20 International. And guess who was the hero of the triumph? Sanath. He slammed two centuries in the ODIs, thus earning the Player of the Series award. He picked up wickets as well to finish a memorable series.

But what capped off the tour was the historic finale on 1 July 2006 when Sanath partnered with Tharanga to a record first wicket stand of 286, which stands till today. There was nothing at stake with the series already sealed, but nobody told Sanath that. Set to chase England's 321 for 7, Sanath and Tharanga set a pace that was difficult to match. They added 286 in just 31.5 overs and the chase was done in just 37.4 overs with 8 wickets to spare. Sanath had made a whopping 152 off 99 balls (20 boundaries and 4 sixes), with the first 50 coming off 26 balls, while his century took 72 balls

[81]'Jayasuriya in Line for Recall', ESPNcricinfo, http://www.espncricinfo.com/engvsl/content/story/249041.html, 1 June 2006.

only! Incidentally, the day, 1 July 2006, was a bad day for English sports in more ways than one. That was also the day champion English fast bowler of the yore, Fred Trueman, had passed away, and in neighbouring Germany, the English football was knocked out of the FIFA World Cup via a penalty shootout by Portugal.

It seemed like things were nicely set up for Sanath to cap off a brilliant career at the 2007 World Cup in West Indies. He seemed to be in the best form of his life indeed. All the troubles of the past few months seemed to be behind him.

'It was a hard time I went through, those six-seven months,' he said after arriving in West Indies for the World Cup. He started out with a rapid 109 off 87 balls against Bangladesh in the league stage with 7 boundaries and 7 sixes. During the course of the knock, he set the record for most sixes, 231, in his ODI career, going past Pakistan's Shahid Afridi. He then followed it up with a second century—his career's 25th—this time against host West Indies in the Super Eight stage in Guyana's Providence Stadium.

Sanath made 115 (10 boundaries and 10 sixes) with the bat and then claimed 3 for 38 with his left-arm spin, earning him the Man of the Match award. The knock saw a different facet of Sanath as he first struggled to make 14 runs from the first 33 balls in the first 15 overs. Then he switched gears, racing to 50 off the next 14 balls and getting a century off another 39. This performance was enough for Jayawardene to hail his teammate as a man key for his campaign. 'He is one of the assets on this team and we hope that he will continue to perform in this manner for the rest of the tournament,' said Jayawardene.[82]

---

[82]'Sri Lanka Outplay Hosts', https://www.dailymail.co.uk/sport/cricket/article-446073/Sri-Lanka-outplay-hosts.html, 2 April 2007.

For Sanath himself, this was amongst the best knocks of his career. 'It is up there among the best because the wicket was not easy early on and I had to be very watchful. But I decided that after the 15th over, we needed some runs and I played my normal type of innings.'[83] It seemed like Sri Lanka was progressing well in the tournament for the first time since the 1996 triumph. Yet again, it was Sanath who was leading the way.

His exploits in the World Cup even forced Coach Moody to come around and compare him with another sporting great, golf's Tiger Woods, in the Australian newspaper *The Age*.[84]

He is a natural sportsman, he's got an incredible eye, and his bat speed is as quick as anyone's bat speed in the game. You talk about Tiger Woods' club head speed, well Jayasuriya is the cricket version of that. You see Gilly (Adam Gilchrist) and guys like that play some amazing shots, but I've seen shots that Jayasuriya plays that no one else could get close to. He's unique. And on his day you can't bowl to him. It is as simple as that, you cannot bowl to him. And the great thing about him is that he's 37, but he's desperate to continue to improve his game without resting on the World Cup in 1996 or anything like that. He is as hungry as he's ever been.

Rich praise also came in from his long-term rivals, Australia's Glenn McGrath and their skipper, Ponting. 'He's a champion one-day player. He's been around a long time and he's got a record. I think they probably don't rely on him as much as they did a couple of

[83]ESPNcricinfo Singles out Jayasuriya', https://www.rte.ie/sport/cricket/2007/0402/216247-srilanka/, 14 June 2007.
[84]'Jayasuriya The Tiger Woods of Cricket: Moody', *The Age*, 15 April 2007.

years ago. But if you can knock him over early, you feel as if you have taken out one of the most dangerous players in world cricket,' praised Ponting.[85]

It seemed like Sanath was a man on a mission in the World Cup. He later revealed that he was driven by the desire to win the World Cup a second time in his career. 'Oh, how I dearly wanted that second World Cup medal,' he said.[86]

Everything was set up nicely for a repeat of the 1996 heroics. The rival of that day in 1996 at Lahore, Australia, stood before Sri Lanka and Sanath once again in the finale of 2007. But that day in Bridgetown, Barbados, another dasher, Gilchrist, had other ideas as he went berserk. Gilchrist's 149 set an improbable target of 282 in 38 overs for Sri Lanka in a rain-curtailed finale. Even then, Sanath provided one last-ditch effort with a 67-ball 63. But it was not to be.

'I wanted to win that final. Unfortunately Adam Gilchrist spoilt my occasion with his breathtaking innings,' he told ESPNcricinfo much later.[87]

Amazingly, for a man with the highest record of sixes in his ODI career, he did not hit even one in the title bout. 'As for not hitting the sixes, the Aussie bowlers probably didn't bowl balls I could have taken advantage of,' he explained.[88]

While his ODI career seemed to have hit a reboot button, the Test match returns were drying progressively. He had scored just 497

---

[85]Ibid.

[86]Interview by Nagraj Gollapudi, 'I'd Like to Play For Another Six Months', ESPIN cricinfo, http://www.espncricinfo.com/magazine/content/story/441258.html, 27 December 2009.

[87]Ibid.

[88]Ibid.

runs since early 2005 in 15 Tests at an average of 19.88 with one 50.

Downward Curve Begins

When England toured Sri Lanka in 2007–08, the media was flush with speculation that Sanath's Test career was finally about to end. Sri Lankan newspaper *Sunday Times* reported that the selectors had given him the option of playing a farewell Test (first of the series) in Kandy against England and then quitting, rather than being dropped.

Sanath himself ended the speculation when he confirmed to the host broadcaster that he had decided to quit Test cricket. 'I will be retiring from Tests after this match,' confirmed Sanath. 'I wanted to end my Test career in Sri Lanka, particularly in Kandy. I will continue playing one-day internationals.'[89] Sanath scored a quick-fire 78 in the second innings of what seemed definitely (external forces willing) like his final Test.

The timing of the decision was unusual because it was the first Test of a three-match series. The announcement was just one Test after Atapattu, too, quit. Sanath's announcement came on a day when Muttiah Muralitharan went past Shane Warne in the leading Test wicket-takers' list of 708.

'This is the right time to retire,' Sanath said. 'There are some young guys coming up, and I wanted to go while on top. Life without cricket will be tough, but I will still be playing one-day cricket and contributing to the team.'[90]

---

[89]'Jayasuriya Announces Retirement from Tests', ESPNcricinfo, http://www.espncricinfo.com/slveng/content/story/323451.html, 3 December 2007.
[90]Ibid.

When the news that Sanath was finally retiring from Test cricket was confirmed, there were tributes flowing from everywhere. Sanath's teammate Sangakkara penned a glowing tribute to his long-time teammate on 9 December 2007 in the British newspaper *The Telegraph*. Some extracts from the letter are produced below:[91]

Sanath Jayasuriya will be missed

When the second Test starts this morning it will herald a new era for Sri Lanka's Test cricket: life without Sunny. For 18 years and 110 Tests, Sanath Jayasuriya has been the face of Sri Lanka's batting and one of the world's most destructive and exhilarating batsmen. We will miss him hugely, as a cricketer and a friend.

I can remember first watching him live as a teenager back in 1996 as Sri Lanka played Kenya in Kandy. He did not make a huge score but he set off like a train, hit the ball with ferocious power and excited us all. He inspired me to take cricket seriously as a professional career, and he inspired a whole generation of children to embrace the game.

Indeed, his impact on Sri Lanka's cricket is not easily overstated.

As a batsman, Sunny was full of quirks and nervous tics. The fidgeting and tapping before each and every delivery is now known to us all. He'd also always bat with a Buddhist Pirith thread around his wrist and before each and every tour he'd visit the temple for blessings.

People have often referred to him as a great 'natural

---

[91]Kumar Sangakkara, 'Sanath Jayasuriya Will Be Missed', *The Telegraph*, 9 December 2007.

talent', but the truth is he worked tremendously hard on his game—both his technique and also his physical fitness.

Quite surprisingly, in ODI cricket, some 23 innings after the 2007 World Cup, Sanath did not go past 50. This lean phase worried the team enough for Sanath to be dropped from the ODI squad for the first time in a long while. He was the second-highest run-getter for Sri Lanka in the World Cup just twelve months ago, but had now been dropped from the side that was to tour West Indies in April 2008.

Sanath was 'hurt' by the snub. He put his head down and headed to play for Mumbai Indians in the inaugural Indian Premier League (IPL). His rich vein of form there made Sri Lankan Minister of Sports Gamini Lokuge push for his recall to the national side. Sanath did return and it proved to be a master stroke.

He returned for the 2008 Asia Cup in Pakistan and hit two centuries—one of them on his thirty-ninth birthday—against Bangladesh and one against his favourite team, India, in the finals when everyone else seemed to fail. Sri Lanka went on to win the Asia Cup and Sanath was back in the mix.

In his twentieth year in international cricket, Sanath was still being driven by self-belief, something that caught the attention of his peers. 'I've been lucky enough to play with him for 10 years now, and his attitude hasn't changed. We have confidence in the game plan he has, and there is a lot for us to learn from watching him,' said Captain Jayawardene to the author.

In December 2009, Sanath was still aiming for one final hurrah at the World Cup in 2011. But he had to battle his lean phase with the bat. In an interview with ESPNcricinfo, Sanath made his goal clear.

'The biggest (goal) is to play the 2011 World Cup. I know Sri Lanka is likely to play about 30 ODIs before the World Cup, but I am not thinking that far. I am only thinking of 5 ODIs at a time, and if I can perform in 3 out those 5, I'm right on track for the next World Cup. I am trying,' he said.[92]

Sanath was moved down the order by the team think-tank and their patience with his lean phase was wearing thin. 'Obviously if the team management wants to send me a message they should be clear about that to me, as they have been in the past,' said Sanath.[93] That clear message came in the new year of 2010 when the selectors, led by the new chairman, Aravinda de Silva, did not retain him in the 20-member elite list. This was another indication that the selectors were finally looking beyond him. However, his recent batting form had been poor. In the ICC World Twenty20 in the West Indies, he averaged only 3.75 from six matches and in his last six ODI matches his highest score was 31.

'The contracts are worked out on the previous year's performances and in Sanath's case, since he had not performed up to expectations, we decided to leave him out,' revealed Aravinda. 'We also allowed him to go to England and play some county cricket to see how he performs.'[94]

Then, he was left out of the 2010 Asia Cup squad; perhaps the strongest indication of him not being considered for the 2011 World Cup. Sri Lanka's Coach Trevor Bayliss had already

---

[92]Interview by Nagraj Gollapudi, 'I'd Like to Play For Another Six Months', 27 December 2009.
[93]Ibid.
[94]Sa'adi Thawfeeq, 'Murali Retains Contract But Jayasuriya Misses Out', ESPNcricinfo, 13 July 2010.

announced that Sanath would be considered in ODIs only as a spinning all-rounder, instead of a specialist opener. Sanath had consistently been left out of the ODI squads since the start of 2010 and had been moved down the order in late 2009.

So, the end was nigh. It was in this phase that Sanath decided to change track and professions completely. Sanath, now a parliamentarian for the ruling party, was picked in the provisional squad of 30 for the ICC Cricket World Cup 2011. But he was not part of the final XV. It had been nearly two years since he had played an ODI for Sri Lanka. Sri Lanka's loss in the World Cup finals, in Mumbai, to co-host India led to a series of changes, especially in the leadership. Their next big assignment was the tour of England. New captain Tillakaratne Dilshan suffered an injury during the English tour in 2011. The other opener, Upul Tharanga, was under a cloud of doping. So the conditions indicated that Sanath would make a dramatic return.

And he did! But Sanath seemed to have had enough of the drama surrounding his place as he announced that he would retire midway through the tour, close to his forty-second birthday.

'The England tour will be my last tour for my country. I will play the first one-day and the Twenty20 match and retire,' he announced. But he did make a parting shot at his critics, 'I am thrilled that the selectors had faith in my fitness.'[95]

'I am still fit enough to play international cricket, though I have not played much one-day matches for the past several months,' he said. 'Age is never an issue. I will be 42. So long as fitness and form is maintained, player burnout is managed properly, there is scope

---

[95]'Sri Lanka Announces International Retirement', ESPNcricinfo, http://www.espncricinfo.com/srilanka/content/story/518500.html, 9 June 2011.

for seniors like myself to represent the country.'[96]

When he finally ended his career, perhaps the most fitting tribute came from one of Sanath's fiercest critic at times, Rex Clementine of *The Island*. In a dispatch from London, Clementine referred to him as Michael Jordan of Sri Lanka in a piece titled 'The legend who made us look stupid'.[97]

> He may have overstayed his welcome, but you have got to respect him for fighting till the last moment. All of us give up too easily, but not Sanath Jayasuriya. Till the last minute, Sanath's enthusiasm never wavered. The argument that he should have been part of the Sri Lanka's World Cup squad is still rumbling and the way he worked out Kevin Pietersen with his left-arm spin in the T20 International at Bristol showed that the old guile is still there.
>
> Sanath, however, may have cooked his goose by seeking political intervention for his selection for 2011 World Cup. Sadly, he never realised that he didn't have to associate with politicians to get what he wanted. Politicians rather needed to hang around with him for he was a global brand name. Sanath Jayasuriya was the Michael Jordan of Sri Lanka. And in the end, it may have been a mistake not to pick him for World Cup, especially given the fact that Sri Lanka did have a specialist left-arm spinner in Rangana Herath in their World Cup squad.

---

[96]Jayasuriya Announces Retirement from Tests', ESPNcricinfo, http://www.espncricinfo.com/slveng/content/story/323451.html, 3 December 2007.
[97]Rex Clementine, 'The Legend Who Makes Us Look Stupid', *The Island*, 27 June 2011.

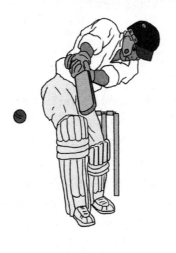

6

Clearly Not His Cup of Tea

There is an interesting anecdote about Sanath's career. He held records for everything that was fast—the fastest half-century off 17 balls (against Pakistan) in 1996, the fastest 150 (against England off 95 balls). But then, he held one more record and that was with regard to his fastest entry and exit from politics.

Much like his first captain, Arjuna Ranatunga, Sanath was a popular personality in Sri Lanka, especially in his home district of Matara. So, he decided to tap into it, and while he was still an active cricketer, Sanath decided to take a plunge into politics. But Sanath was now on the rival side of his former captain Arjuna. Both were the star campaigners for their respective alliances.

In April 2010, Sanath contested from his hometown of Matara District, representing the United People's Freedom Alliance (UPFA). UPFA was born out of an understanding between

Sri Lanka Freedom Party (SLFP) and Janatha Vimukthi Peramuna (JVP) in 2004. The rival of the UPFA was the United National Party (UNP)-led United National Front (UNF).

Sanath received flak from the public after the election commissioner allowed him to cast his vote a day ahead of the official polling day, treating it as a postal vote. It was said that Sanath had no legitimate grounds for asking to be allowed to vote in advance. Sanath was leaving early to play for Mumbai Indians in the IPL, something that did not go down well with the critics who felt he was going away for personal gains rather than for the country.

Rex Clementine, writing for *The Island,* noted in 2011 in a dispatch from London that it was hardly a surprise that he took a plunge into politics.[98]

> It was no surprise when Sanath Jayasuriya took to politics. He loved politics and in turn politicians liked to be seen around with him and most of his wishes were granted. Sadly, what's not known is that on most occasions he sought political assistance not for himself, but for his teammates. In 2002, when the selectors opted to rest Marvan Atapattu from the third Test against Zimbabwe at Asgiriya, Jayasuriya directly took up the matter with then Minister of Sports Johnston Fernando. Eventually Atapattu was reinstated and mind you the selectors were sacked. It was clear from those days that he will take up politics one day. But what was not known then was that he will take it up while playing and representing SLFP. There was this belief that he was an UNPer.

[98]Ibid.

Sanath secured the most number of preferential votes, polling 74,352 votes. He bested his rival Buddhika Pathirana from the UNP, who got just over 50,000 votes. Sanath knew his constituency, Matara, quite well. He had grown up in the area and had done his schooling here. 'I know the area well. This place needs development. I am going to help the people. I have already campaigned for the president in the last elections. He requested me to contest this election. I was pushed to this decision after an exhaustive study,' Sanath said.[99]

Sanath's stop-start international career did not deter him from entering politics. In fact, it added another dimension to the superstar phenomenon that he was in the Emerald Island. Then a forty-year-old, Sanath was dropped from the Sri Lanka ODI squad, but he insisted that he had not given up on his playing career, despite his entry into politics.

'I have no plans to retire from international cricket at this stage as I believe I can successfully balance the workload of playing for Sri Lanka while also serving the people of Matara as an MP. Also since I am not playing Test Cricket, I will have enough time for politics,' Sanath told reporters after his win from Matara.[100] 'It has been an honour representing Sri Lanka on the cricket field during the past 21 years and after careful consideration I believe now is the right time for me to serve the people of Matara.'

'I have nothing to earn from the politics. But I can work for the people who loved me a lot. It is the bounden duty to serve the people, in return, for what they did for me to come to this

---

[99]Sanath Jayasuriya blogspot, http://sanath189.blogspot.com/2010/02/, 25 February 2010.
[100]'Sri Lanka's Jayasuriya Enters Politics', http://www.stuff.co.nz/sport/cricket/3346956/Sri-Lankas-Jayasuriya-enters-politics, 18 February 2010.

position,' he added. 'When the UPFA invited me to contest for general elections I accepted it since this is a golden opportunity to work for the people wholeheartedly,' Sanath told the local newspaper *Daily News.*[101]

But this decision of Sanath did not please his one-time mentor Arjuna. The former captain was now on the side of the rival presidential candidate, Sarath Fonseka, also a former army chief. Arjuna's contention was that Sanath or any active cricketer should not join politics. Arjuna entered politics during the 2005 general elections and went on to become a minister. But Arjuna quickly fell out of favour with President Mahinda Rajapaksa.

Incidentally, the man to give Sanath an all-clear from SLC was none other than Arjuna's brother, Nishantha, who was the secretary of the Board. Sanath needed the clearance to contest elections as he was still an active cricketer. However, the decision to enter politics split his cricket fans right in the middle. Sanath was now no longer a certainty in the Sri Lankan shorter formats as the younger players started getting preference.

'When you play as a cricketer, they all love you as a unit. When you go to a (political) party, naturally it's divided. So I need to face that. Just before I came to politics, I thought of that, and I know it's going to be a half-half situation—unless you're a very big fan of mine,' Sanath told BBC in Colombo in 2011. 'I'm not regretting coming to politics. But the fans got divided, that's true.'[102]

---

[101]'Jayasuriya to Take On Ranatunga in Politics', https://www.thehindu.com/sport/cricket/Jayasuriya-to-take-on-Ranatunga-in-politics/article16814888.ece, 16 February 2010.

[102]'Sanath Jayasuriya: Master-blaster's Exciting Last Stand', https://www.bbc.com/news/world-south-asia-13716558, 9 June 2011.

Making a Pitch for Return

There was feverish speculation over whether Sanath would be recalled in time for the ICC Cricket World Cup in 2011. After all, the tournament was going to be co-hosted by Bangladesh, India and Sri Lanka. Another legend of Sanath's vintage, Muttiah Muralitharan, also part of the famous 1996 World Cup champion squad, was going to hang his boots post the 2011 World Cup.

It was hoped that Sanath would be given one final go at the World Cup, much like his famous teammate. But it was not to be. The national selectors left him out of the squad for the ICC Cricket World Cup 2011. Sri Lanka lost to fellow host India in a high-scoring finale in Mumbai. There were a number of fallouts of that win, most notably being the resignation of Captain Kumar Sangakkara.

SLC, meanwhile, entered yet another phase of uncertainty. The political changes within the SLC were forever a cause of disagreement for the growth of cricket in that country. Yet again, there was an interim committee that found its way into the administration of cricket in that country. At forty-two, Sanath was then the oldest active player in international cricket. But there were reports that the teammates, especially the now powerful duo of Sangakkara and Mahela Jayawardene, did not look at his entry into politics favourably.

Sanath, however, was quick to deny any such problem. 'No, they never said anything about (my) coming to politics,' he said, 'I am not a person who is interfering politics into the cricket. I am always like a normal human being, a normal member of the team.'[103]

---

[103]Ibid.

In the autumn of his cricketing career, a new set of selectors gave Sanath a fresh go for the national side. Sri Lanka was touring England at the time and the selectors picked Sanath for the tour almost against all odds. This selection was also necessitated because of another controversy brewing within the squad in England. Fellow opener Upul Tharanga had failed a dope test and was all set to face punitive action for the same. Regular skipper Tillakaratne Dilshan was injured, while there were several niggles within the squad. In such a scenario, it became easy for the selectors to go for Sanath. Sanath was thus all set to become the first active cricketer to play international cricket even while being an elected parliamentarian.

Finishing on his Own Terms

But hours after being picked to play for Sri Lanka again, Sanath arranged for an impromptu media conference. The media turned up in large numbers because they thought it was organized to share his joy of returning to international cricket. Sanath had not played ODI cricket for Sri Lanka since December 2009 and had not played a Twenty20 international for over a year. He had not been picked in Sri Lanka's World Cup squad and had failed to secure a contract with a franchise in that year's IPL, leading many to believe he would not play international cricket again.

'I invited you here not to share the happiness of my being selected to play for Sri Lanka again, but to announce my decision to end my international career of more than 20 years,' said Sanath in a surprise announcement at the Premadasa Stadium in Colombo even as his other teammates were busy training.

Sanath was picked for the full limited-overs series in England, but he decided enough was enough. 'I consider it a privilege to have represented Sri Lanka to bring glory to my country and the town of Matara where I come from. The selectors picked me for the whole series but it is my personal decision to retire midway (through the series).'[104]

The British press, however, was waiting for Sanath for a different reason. Not just Sanath, Sri Lanka as a whole was in the news for other reasons. The civil war of nearly 35 years against the LTTE had ended in 2009. There was a massive outcry worldwide about the human rights violation by the Sri Lankan army. President Mahinda Rajapaksa faced widespread criticism for the way the war had ended. Sanath, as a ruling party MP, faced dual responsibility, not just padding up for the national team, but also for his country on the world stage.

Noted columnist Andy Bull, writing for *The Guardian* in his column, 'The Spin', on 21 June 2011 tore into his selection for the tour, not entirely for cricketing reasons.

> Disgrace. What a tediously familiar word; stripped of significance by its overuse, shorn of force by its frequent repetition. Read it again. Roll it around your tongue. Feel its heat and taste its weight, because I am about to use it and I do not want to do so lightly. In the next seven days England are due to play two games against Sri Lanka which will be used as valedictory matches for Sanath Jayasuriya, who has been recalled to the squad at the age of 41. Jayasuriya's selection is a disgrace and the idea of playing cricket against a team that includes him is a disgrace.

---

[104]'Jayasuriya to Retire from International Game in England', *Independent*, 10 June 2011.

Only a fool thinks that sport and politics do not mix.

In April 2010 Jayasuriya was elected as the MP for Matara in southern Sri Lanka. He represents the United People's Freedom Alliance, the party of President Mahinda Rajapaksa. Jayasuriya's recall was ordered by Rajapaksa's government. It is an overtly political decision.

But even if there was any cricketing logic to his inclusion, his selection would still be unacceptable. Jayasuriya is an elected representative of a government who, according to a United Nations report published this April, could be responsible for the deaths of 40,000 Tamil citizens during the final campaign of the civil war in late 2008 and early 2009.[105]

Affectionately referred to as Sana, the Deveni Meheyuma (second innings) of politics was now putting the former captain in the firing line. But he was equal to the task.

'(World) should realize that the Sri Lankan government has stopped one of the worst terrorist organisations in the world. I am 41 years old. Thirty years of my life, we went through a terrible time in Sri Lanka. Anybody can come into my country now and walk anywhere without fear,' Sanath said.[106]

But England pulled out of the 2003 World Cup match in Zimbabwe and forfeited their points. The British columnists in 2011 were now questioning the hypocrisy of playing against a team with a player (Sanath) who was part of a government that had been accused of similar crimes by the world at large. The English tour ended without any untoward incident for Sanath as he was

---

[105] Andy Bull, *The Guardian*, 'The Spin', 21 June 2011.

[106] 'Sanath Jayasuriya: Master-blaster's Exciting Last Stand', BBC News, 9 June 2011.

part of the squad just for the one-off Twenty20 International and the first ODI.

Getting his Hands Dirty

Sanath quickly rose in the ranks of the SLFP. He was now also the main organizer for the SLFP in his hometown of Matara and the Matara District Development Committee chairman.

Then, in October 2013, he joined the cabinet of President Mahinda Rajapaksa. He was one of the nine deputy ministers to be sworn in by the president. Sanath was handed the Ministry of Postal Services.

In June 2014, Sanath got involved in another imbroglio—this time a political one. He was accused by the opposition Marxist party, Janatha Vimukthi Peramuna (JVP), of leading an attack on the students of the University of Ruhuna. The students were protesting a government plan to hold an annual development exhibition 'Deyata Kirula' within the university in the district of Matara. But Sanath strongly refuted the allegations.

The students claimed that on 2 June 2014, at around 2 p.m., a group of nearly 300, including Sanath, Provincial Council Minister D.V. Upul and Aruna Gunaratne, had staged the attack. They accused the protestors of possessing clubs and batons.

'I am the area (Matara) MP. I was only participating in a protest organized by the local residents against the university students. I did not attack anyone and was not present at the time of the alleged assault,' denied Sanath.[107]

[107]'Jayasuriya Accused of Attacking Lankan Undergraduates', *The Times of India*, 4 June 2014.

Even though the tension was extinguished by the Matara police, the opposition continued to accuse Sanath for the attack. The locals wanted the exhibition to take place within the varsity premises, but the students were opposed to the idea. The students felt that it would destroy the aesthetic beauty of the university.

JVP Secretary Tilvyn Silva led the attack of his party on Sanath. He presented photographic evidence of Sanath being part of the mob that allegedly attacked the students. Silva accused Sanath of digging graves for the students. 'What they want is to create disturbances and sabotage activities at the university, which they have already accomplished, as the campus has been closed indefinitely,' said Silva.[108]

This violence also had a ripple effect on Sanath's standing in Matara. The Matara cricket ground had been named after him, but the UNP demanded that it be removed forthwith. 'I will make a request to the Matara Municipal Council to change the name of Sanath Jayasuriya sports ground into its previous name St. Servasious because Deputy Minister Jayasuriya had assaulted university students—an act unsuitable for a minister,' UNP Matara District Parliamentarian Mangala Samaraweera said in a news conference.[109]

Sanath continued to face difficulties from his own setup. A rival seemed to emerge from within the SLFP for the district of Matara. Fellow Minister Mervyn Silva's son Malaka Silva announced that

---

[108]'Sri Lanka: Master Blaster Sanath Jayasuriya Rips Open Student's Head, Sri Lanka Brief, http://srilankabrief.org/2014/06/sri-lanka-master-blaster-sanath-jayasuriya-rips-open-students-heads-jvp/, 3 June 2014.
[109]'Sanath on Slippery Wicket', Daily Mirror, http://www.dailymirror.lk/article/sanath-on-slippery-wicket-48048.html, 5 June 2015.

he would start his political journey from Matara. The issue of the student protest and the alleged attacks on them had just about died down when the new rival for Matara cropped up.

'The people who live in Matara are very intelligent. They use their brain well before voting and use their preference. They come to a decision about the candidates based on their history, the service rendered by them etc., before voting. There are various kinds of people who come to Matara from time to time. Some candidates came during the last southern election period too,' said Sanath in an interview to the *Daily Mirror*.[110]

Malaka was someone with a chequered past. He was seen as a 'playboy', the son of a wealthy politician. He was often seen going to nightclubs and buying new cars. He had eight bodyguards and possessed a car worth ₹400 lakh. With such a background, Malaka was the centre of attacks from his rivals, especially Sanath.

But Malaka was determined to enter the political arena from Matara. 'Well, I can say I am receiving a very positive response from the public about that. I get lots of encouragement via phone calls and discussions with the ordinary citizens,' said Malaka to *Daily Mirror*.[111] In fact, he noted, 'Only one person opposed his coming to Matara and that is Deputy Minister Sanath Jayasuriya.'[112]

Following are excerpts of an interview that Malaka gave to *Daily Mirror*. The flamboyant Malaka accused Sanath of many things and this interview set the stage for a bitter battle for Matara.

---

[110]'Malaka and I Are Poles Apart', *Daily Mirror*, 6 July 2014.
[111]Dayaseeli Liyanage, 'Only Jayasuriya Opposes My Entry into Politics', 16 July 2014.
[112]Ibid.

Mr Jayasuriya said that you and he are poles apart—that you two are like the sky and the ground. Where do you stand? The sky or the ground?

Matara people have told me that Sanath Jayasuriya has his head in the clouds. But I am of course someone who is more grounded. I can coexist with anybody at any level.

I was never elevated to the sky. Politicians who live in the sky will one day realize that they are too high above the ground. When people give their verdict, they will finally understand their folly.

Just talk to the people of the Matara district, they will tell you who stands where.

Mr Jayasuriya also stated that he won't let anyone bring terror and violence to the Matara district. Do you think that terror will follow you to Matara?

What is terror? Is it going to a nightclub 'terror'? Is it having a problem with someone else? I don't understand. I am entering Matara peacefully. I am not someone who goes backwards.

Have you met Mr Jayasuriya?

Yes, I have met him in nightclubs. He is a minister and he patronizes nightclubs. At least, I am not a minister.

Are the two of you friends?

We are not exactly friends but we talk when we see each other. He also has a restaurant.

Mr Jayasuriya has said that he is not ready to do politics if an outsider comes to Matara.

Well, that means he cannot face a challenge. He is already afraid. That is a weakness. If you are politician, you should be ready to face any challenge. This is what happens when you are just a namesake politician. How can he face the opposition if that is his attitude?

In his response, Sanath was as caustic while talking to the same newspaper.

Isn't it a challenge for you if Malaka Silva would come?
There is no challenge for me at all. This character and I are poles apart. Those who had acted like thugs, would not have achieved anything according to history. What he has done in the past is not a patch on mine. The people in Matara will not allow them to unleash terror in Matara like Kelaniya.

Malaka says that he had a lot of relatives in Matara. According to him, Matara is a vote-base for him. Isn't it a challenge for you?
No, not at all. When I first contested for Matara, I came first in the district. The people are aware that this Matara lad had brought fame to the country. They have a high regard for me as their relative. I do not want to create new relatives. We all are human beings. It is the same blood that circulates in our bodies. People know. 'Those who live with the dogs, have to go out with the fleas also.'

Do you think Malaka Silva is an outsider to Matara?
Well, I have not seen Malaka Silva living in Matara. I, on the other hand, was born and raised in Matara; I went to school in Matara my whole student life. I first played for Matara before I came to play in Colombo. My identity is in Matara. Anybody can come to Matara and do what they wish. However, I am not going to allow anybody to bring violence

and terror to Matara. I don't think the people of Matara wish for terror, violence, guns and bombs in their hometown. They want to continue to live in peace and harmony.

If Malaka does come to Matara, will you shake hands with him and accept him?
I don't know at which level he is going to enter the political arena of Matara. I am the party organizer for Matara. I don't expect an outsider to take the Matara seat. I can't do politics like that. If someone else tries to take my seat, I can't do my political work. However, no such thing has happened yet. This was a self-proclamation by him.

Bowing Out

When Rajapaksa was voted out of power in January 2015, Sanath made a reverse sweep as he continued in Parliament under the new regime of National Unity. The president then was Maithripala Sirisena, who headed a new coalition with Prime Minister Ranil Wickremasinghe.

But the constant bickering of politics got to Sanath. He finally quit his position and did not contest in the general elections in 2015. He was deputy minister of local government and rural development just before his resignation.

'As the deputy minister of post in the Mahinda Rajapaksa government, I could not even get the buildings of the Matara Post Office painted,' Sanath lamented in response to a question posed by a media personnel.'[113] Although I was the chairman of the District

---

[113]'I Could Not Even Get Matara Post Office Painted: Sanath', https://www.onlanka.com/news/i-could-not-even-get-matara-post-office-painted-sanath.html, 13 August 2015.

Development Committee, I was unable to initiate any development work in Matara. I was merely a figurehead agreeing to development projects put forward by others. During the MR (Rajapaksa) era, there were permanent hoardings in the centre of Matara which even the mayor did not dare to remove,' he added.[114]

7

Donning a New Hat, Yet Again

It was hard to imagine that Sanath had finally finished his international career in 2011. He was now a member of parliament, but was still plying his trade in domestic cricket. He continued playing domestic cricket for another year. In fact, he was so multifaceted that he was a parliamentarian, a dancer on a reality TV show in India and a cricketer in Sri Lanka.

Sanath, the cricketer, was, however, still very much in heavy demand when it came to Twenty20 cricket. The clearest indication of that came in July 2012 when, at the age of forty-three—considered old in many ways for playing cricket—he was one of the top buys in the draft for the inaugural edition of the Sri Lanka Premier League (SLPL). Sanath fetched the maximum price of US$35,000 by the franchise of Kandurata.

So, his cricket career may have ended, but the lure of Sanath the superstar was still very much there. He still commanded a price that many of his peers—in fact, many of his younger teammates—could only dream of. He was fit, agile on the field and was still striking the ball well.

Right after the SLPL, Sanath exhibited another facet of his personality when he donned the role of a cricket diplomat. International cricket in Pakistan had been halted post the horrific attacks on the Sri Lankan squad in Lahore in 2009. Cricketers were scared to make the trip to Pakistan for obvious reasons. Pakistan themselves shifted their 'home' to United Arab Emirates (UAE) in order to fulfil their commitments. In the midst of all this, in October 2012, Sanath led an International XI, managed by former West Indies batsman Alvin Kallicharan. The squad was to play two exhibition Twenty20 matches against a Pakistan Stars XI at the National Stadium in Karachi. The squad included a number of recently retired players like West Indies' trio of Ricardo Powell, Jermaine Lawson and Adam Sanford, alongside South African pacemen Andre Nel and Nantine Hayward.

The games had been organized by the minister of sports of the province of Sindh, Dr Mohammad Ali Shah. So the tour definitely had political overtones. Being a MP himself, Sanath led from the front in the efforts.

Political Pawn

Politics and Sri Lankan cricket go hand in hand. No Sri Lankan squad chosen can take the field without the express approval of the minister of sports. In fact, the selection panel itself is appointed by the minister of sports of the day.

So, it was hardly a surprise when in January 2013, the minister of sports at the time, Mahindananda Aluthgamage, decided to make changes to the National Selection Panel and also increased the number of selectors to five.

Aluthgamage was a member of the ruling UPFA. So he did not have to look beyond his partyman and fellow MP Deshbandhu Sanath Jayasuriya. In fact, Sanath was a late addition to a list of nominees sent to the Aluthgamage by Sri Lanka Cricket (SLC). It was easy for the minister to approve the choices, especially because of the presence of Sanath. So, 19 months after his last appearance for Sri Lanka and six months after his last competitive game, Sanath was back in the sport he loved, albeit in a completely different role.

Sanath was to be joined by his ex-teammates, including former fast bowlers Pramodya Wickramasinghe and Eric Upashantha, along with former batsman Chaminda Mendis. Hemantha Wickramaratne was the only selector to receive a second consecutive term, having also served in the previous panel under former fast bowler Ashantha de Mel.

What was interesting was that Sanath's panel did not have a specific term for their role. At that stage, Sri Lanka used to have a new selection panel every year, but this time the minister of sports made an exception. While it was not explicitly mentioned, it was clear that Sanath's presence was the reason.

'Under the sports law, it's the minister's prerogative to hand down a term for the selectors, but he hasn't done that this time,' a spokesperson for the sports ministry told ESPNcricinfo. 'If the selectors are doing a good job, they can continue.'[115]

In fact, the process of appointing the selection panel was in complete contravention of the suggestion made to SLC by

---

[115] Andrew Fernando, 'Jayasuriya Named Chairman of Selectors', ESPNcricinfo, 28 January 2013.

the former ICC Chief Executive Haroon Lorgat to keep politics divorced from sports in the country. This was a way of ending the political influence in Sri Lankan cricket. Lorgat had conducted a review for SLC and had suggested to make changes to the sports law.

But it would have been so ironic had that happened because one of the biggest beneficiaries of the interference of a politician was Sanath himself. In fact, Sanath made a return to the ODI squad in 2008 at the insistence of the then minister of sports.

Sanath was now in charge and his first job was to choose a new Test and ODI captain. Mahela Jayawardene, a reluctant leader, had stepped down and there was a void. Two other senior pros, Kumar Sangakkara and Tillakaratne Dilshan, were also not keen to take up the role. The clearest choice was the Twenty20 captain, Angelo Mathews. But here again, the minister of sports had made it clear that he would prefer two separate captains. Hence, Sanath's panel had their task cut out.

But even before they could get down to the task, there was another roadblock. The only selector who was retained, Wickramaratne, stepped down from the panel. He was then replaced by former Test captain, Hashan Tillakaratne, in an announcement made by Sanath himself.

What made the announcement even more curious was that Tillakaratne was the member of the opposition, UNP, and the provincial council. Tillakaratne had been one of the nominees sent to the minister of sports by SLC, but had not been picked earlier.

Tillakaratne was to now be a full-time selector, alongside Wickramasinghe, while Sanath, Upashantha and Mendis were to don part-time roles. What made his appointment interesting was the fact that he had alleged political interference in the SLC elections. With such a background, Tillakaratne's elevation raised questions of possible political slugfest in selection meetings.

However, Sanath dismissed such ideas. 'We're not concerned with the politics of either party on this panel. What we are concerned with is Sri Lanka's cricket and that will be our top priority. We should thank the minister of sports for choosing someone like Hashan, who has played for Sri Lanka and also been a good captain. The minister of sports has given us the freedom to act independently of political affiliations and it was encouraging to hear that. We will stay focused on improving Sri Lanka's cricket.'[116]

That Sanath was stepping into a minefield was clear not just from the political overtones to his appointment, but also from the problems within the squad itself. Senior pros, Jayawardene and Sangakkara, were at the centre of a controversy. Both were rumoured to be on the firing line of Sanath's panel for different reasons.

Jayawardene's confidential letter to SLC in his last stint as the captain was leaked to the media in December 2012. He had publicly made comments in his reaction saying he had 'lost all confidence in dealing with SLC' as a result of the leak. SLC, in response, issued a statement saying Jayawardene's comments would be reviewed by the executive committee.

There were also rumours that Sangakkara would be dropped as an 'act of revenge' by Sanath. Sangakkara was the captain when Sanath had been dropped from the limited-overs squads.

But Sanath was at pains to dismiss such conspiracy theories. 'I've already said that we need the senior cricketers in the setup,' he

[116]Andrew Fernando, 'Tillakaratne Joins SLC Selection Panel', ESPNcricinfo, 30 January 2013.

said. 'Without senior players, it's very difficult for the youngsters to go forward. As a selection panel, we haven't had discussions yet, but the seniors have a role to play. We haven't been appointed to cut Mahela or Sangakkara from the team; we're here to make good selections. It's good to introduce one or two youngsters in the team, but you can't make big changes at once. We will work step-by-step with the seniors.'[117]

True to his word, Sanath's panel retained the two superstars of Sri Lankan cricket, even while handing the reigns of the side to the younger Mathews and Dinesh Chandimal. Sri Lanka was truly moving into an era of transition with the change in leadership.

Mathews had been Sri Lanka's Twenty20 captain since the end of the World Twenty20 in 2012. But in a clear indication of bowing to the minister of sports' wishes, Sanath's panel decided to split the captaincy roles. Chandimal was handed the Twenty20 role, while Mathews became the new Test and ODI skipper.

'We thought that it would be too much for Angelo to give him the Twenty20 captaincy as well, as we wanted to allow him to concentrate on the Tests and ODIs,' Sanath said. 'We thought the best person for the Twenty20 captaincy was Dinesh Chandimal, who has a long future in the game. He will also get some experience of captaining Sri Lanka in case Angelo gets injured.'[118]

Few other senior players like Thilan Samaraweera and Prasanna Jayawardene were dropped and it was a clear indication that Sanath's committee was keen to look ahead rather than back.

---

[117]Andrew Fernando, 'Jayasuriya Promises Fair Selection', ESPNcricinfo, 30 January 2013.
[118]Andrew Fernando, 'Matthew Targets Improved Rankings', ESPNcricinfo, 14 February 2013.

Brokering Peace

If Sanath thought that his job was easy, then he had it wrong. Around 23 national players were engaged in direct confrontation with the SLC over their annual contracts. This crisis hit Sri Lankan cricket right before Bangladesh was to tour the island. An ultimatum from the SLC meant that the players had to sign the contracts if they had to play any form of international cricket again.

A meeting between the two parties proved inconclusive as both sides were stuck to their stance. Sanath's panel had nothing do with the matter, but they were pressed into service because the SLC advised selectors to not select a player who hadn't signed the annual contracts. Furthermore, the players were also barred from using any SLC facility until they signed the contracts.

In all, around 60 national players had been in the firing line, because they had demanded a 25 per cent share in the Board's earnings from the ICC events. The SLC had been paying the players the 25 per cent fee since 2003, but a decade later, the cash-strapped SLC had dropped that from the annual contract saying that the national players were already well-paid.

With a potential crisis looming large, Sanath was pressed into service to solve the impasse. It was the day after the deadline expired—3 March—that Sanath stepped in. This was a personal attempt by Sanath to break the deadlock. SLC president, Upali Dharmadasa, had refused to have any more discussions with the players and the minister of sports had ordered to pick a debutant team to play against the touring Bangladesh. The move proved successful as a relieved Sanath announced after over two hours of protracted discussions with the players: 'The players have decided to put their country first and sign the original contract. Once they sign, they will be considered for selection for the Bangladesh series.'[119]

Sanath said that while the players had come around, they wanted to have further discussions on the contentious clause of ICC's share with SLC. 'In the meantime when the ICC events come, the players will talk to the SLC what they are going to do about the players' guarantee money,' he announced.[120] But despite Sanath's announcement, SLC secretary Nishantha Ranatunga was unwilling to call the crisis closed until contracts were signed. 'What I've heard from Sanath is that the players will sign, but a full resolution hasn't been reached,' reacted Ranatunga.[121]

The players had 24 hours from the time they met Sanath to sign the contract. If they wanted to be considered for international cricket, they had to sign. SLC contributed to the crisis by not recognizing players' managers and associations. The other contentious clauses were related to not paying players salaries during the IPL. In addition to this, the new contracts also had clauses scrapping spouses' business-class travel once every year and a performance linked payment as per the ICC rankings. It was, therefore, a tense 24 hours.

Thankfully, the crisis blew over when the players signed on the dotted line on 4 March 2013. It was Sanath's triumph that a four-tiered contracts list was successfully issued.

The 'top pay' category has been expanded from five players to seven, with Mathews, Nuwan Kulasekara and Rangana Herath

---

[119]Andrew Fernando, 'Jayasuriya Steps In to Help Contracts Settlement,' ESPNcricinfo, 3 March 2013.
[120]Ibid.
[121]Ibid.

joining Jayawardene, Sangakkara and Lasith Malinga in the top tier. SLC CEO Ajit Jayasekara announced that the matter was considered closed.

Sanath was the happiest and wanted to move past the crisis. 'I explained to the players as the chairman of selectors, what we are trying to do in Sri Lankan cricket. They accepted that and were happy, and said that they would try. In the end they wanted to play for Sri Lanka.'[122]

With the issue settled, the focus then moved to Sanath's role as chairman of selectors. He had a tough balancing act to pull off as a ruling party MP and chief selector, while also keeping the minister of sports in the loop.

But it was not long before Sanath slipped. He made the first wrong move when they picked the son of a central minister in the national squad for the one-off Twenty20 International against the touring Bangladesh side. Sanath's panel attracted biting criticism from the media. The player in question was all-rounder Ramith Rambukwella, son of media and information minister, Keheliya Rambukwella.

'Ramith is a left-hand batsman who bowls right arm off-spin, who can clear the boundaries and can hit hard,' defended Sanath. 'He's someone who can play Twenty20 cricket in the middle order, and you need players like that in this format. We're bringing him on as a batting all-rounder who can bowl off-spin.'[123]

---

[122]Andrew Fernando. 'Sri Lanka Contracts Crisis Ends', ESPNcricinfo, 4 March 2013.

[123]Andrew Fernando, 'Jayasuriya Defends Selection of Minister's Son', ESPNcricinfo, http://www.espncricinfo.com/sri-lanka-v-bangladesh-2013/content/story/627269.html, 30 March 2013.

Rambukwella, aged twenty-one at the time, has been playing local cricket for two years. His returns as a player were not exactly flash, as he had hit just two half-centuries in 28 innings across all formats. At that stage, he had scored 135 runs at an average of 16.87 in List A (one-day) games and 122 at 17.42 in Twenty20s. He had been more successful with the ball, having taken 10 wickets at an average of 23.60 in List A and 8 wickets in Twenty20s at an economy-rate of 7.28. His reputation as a big-hitter was developed during his time for Colombo's Royal College.

'We don't just bring in players who perform, we also bring in players with talent,' Sanath explained. 'There are plenty of players who haven't performed that well in club matches, but have played well in internationals. I've seen a lot of players like that. I'm not saying you can get picked even if you don't bat well in domestic cricket, I'm saying if you are talented, or you've made runs in the past, we will give those players an opportunity. We will consider any player. They don't just have to be under 23, even 28 to 30-year-olds are considered, and we will try to take those players to the place they need to go.'[124]

Rambukwella has featured in just two Twenty20 Internationals for Sri Lanka since his selection for the first time during Sanath's tenure. He does not even appear close to being picked again by Sri Lanka in any other format. It was very clear, therefore, that Sanath's tenure as chief selector was going to be remembered for all the wrong reasons. He would have to not only ward off political interference in his work, but at the same time also plan for life after the senior pros were gone. Sanath's panel laid some clear parameters, which they hoped would chart the path ahead.

---

[124]Ibid.

'Our policy is to give as much exposure to youngsters but, in this regard, we must also be careful as to how we go about it,' he said. 'In Tests and ODIs, we cannot experiment too much with youngsters, we need the three seniors around. As you may have noticed, it is the seniors who have won us matches in these two formats over the last couple of years.'[125]

While in cricket, Sanath was plotting to create a legacy; in politics, he was being given fresh responsibility as minister for postal services. Elsewhere, Sri Lankan cricket was suffering from another problem with the much heralded head coach, Graham Ford, stepping down. While the reason for his resignation remained a mystery, no one could deny that it had to do with politics infesting Sri Lankan cricket. Sanath was named as part of the panel that was to pick the new coach, adding yet another responsibility on his shoulders apart from the work that he was already doing. Thus began the most difficult yet the most profitable year of Sanath's tenure as chief selector.

The problems started with the resignation of Ford, but it continued thereafter. He started by publicly questioning the work ethics of one of his top all-rounders, Thisara Perera. A hard-hitting seam-bowling all-rounder, Perera was in the firing line because he had opted to go away to play in Australia's domestic Twenty20 franchise competition, Big Bash League (BBL). Sanath was scathing in his comments. 'We are not giving him permission to play in the Big Bash. He has to work and stay in Sri Lanka,' Sanath told ESPNcricinfo. 'The reason is poor form. He's been in very poor form with his bowling and batting. He needs to work on some

---

[125]Sa'adi Thawfeeq, 'Jayasuriya Confirms Malinga will Miss Zimbabwe Tour', ESPNcricinfo, 30 August 2013.

things with the coaches in Sri Lanka. Before he thinks of playing for Big Bash and all these things, he needs to do the work in Sri Lanka, if he wants to become a good all-rounder. That's what the selectors think.'[126]

Stepping in to Douse the Fire

Then, there was another crisis with the player contracts. This was the third straight year the senior players and the SLC were at loggerheads over the same issue.

Sanath once again emerged as a key figure in the negotiations between the two parties. He had successfully mediated a solution in 2013 after having first taken over as chief selector. In March 2014, he was pressed into service again, this time also on the issue of the ICC event share. The squad was on its way to Bangladesh, but before they left for the tour, they handed a letter to Sanath detailing their demands.

'I could not hand over the letter to SLC but I very clearly informed all officials and CEO Ashley de Silva of the players' wishes,' Sanath told *Daily Mirror*.[127]

Incidentally, it was Sanath, who, as captain in 2003, had led the demand for a share in ICC's events income for the players. So this was a topic that was close to his heart. 'After all, SLC gets all that income because of the cricket the players play,' he said.

As part of a peace mission, Sanath flew with the SLC president,

---

[126] Andrew Fernando, 'Jayasuriya Questions Perera's Work Ethic', ESPNcricinfo, 3 January 2014.

[127] Channaka de Silva, 'SLC Divided on Player Contract Issue', *Daily Mirror*, 6 March 2014.

Jayantha Dharmadasa, and secretary, Ranatunga, to pacify the players. A dialogue was the only way forward in the impasse. The problem started even before the tour to Bangladesh began in January 2014, when the squad refused to sign the squad terms for the upcoming ICC World Twenty20.

The squad terms essentially granted rights to the ICC for using player images during the tournament. But the players wanted to be paid for these rights as ICC shared its revenue with the SLC. It required deft work by Sanath to avert the crisis, as both parties were firm in their stance.

'I was at a meeting with the president (Dharmadasa) till eleven o'clock last night. Angelo (Mathews, Test and ODI captain) called me and said that they needed to meet me urgently before they took the final decision on whether to sign the terms or not. He told me that they would come to SLC headquarters at 1 a.m. in order to take a decision and then leave for Bangladesh. So, I went home at 11 and set the alarm and had a little sleep before going to cricket board office a little after 1 in the morning,' Sanath was quoted as saying in the *Daily Mirror*.[128]

Several rounds of discussion meant that Mathews and Chandimal first agreed to sign the contract and then changed their minds. It then required further persuasion by Sanath before the players finally agreed to the squad terms of the ICC. Therefore, the crisis was slowly building, but this time in March 2014, it was a matter between SLC and the players.

The SLC top brass, along with Sanath, CEO Ashley de Silva, secretary Ranatunga and vice-president Mohan de Silva, met up

---

[128]http://www.dailymirror.lk/mobile/article/jayasuriya-averts-crisis-in-midnight-drama-at-slc-42088.html

with the 17 players who were offered contracts. The group also included seniors like Jayawardene, Sangakkara, Malinga, Rangana Herath and Nuwan Kulasekara. The outcome of the meeting was successful as SLC made it known via a media release later:[129]

> Sri Lanka Cricket wishes to announce that the office bearers of SLC met with the national team players today and had a discussion with regard to the player contract payments. The players expressed their concerns and the office bearers stated their point of view on the subject, and there was an exchange of views between both parties. The office bearers will communicate the views exchanged at the meeting to the members of the executive committee tomorrow for a final decision.

Sanath was the happiest because all the hard work put in behind the scenes was finally bearing fruit. 'Exactly what that compensation is, is up to the board,' he said. 'I can't promise anything because I don't make that decision.'[130]

But Sanath, the mediator, very soon became the bone of contention with the very senior players he had been siding with till recently. Just before the ICC World Twenty20 in Bangladesh, both Jayawardene and Sangakkara used different methods to announce that they would retire from Twenty20 Internationals after the tournament. Sangakkara told *Sunday Island* before his departure,

---

[129]'Player Contract Payments: Office Bearers Met with Players', http://www.srilankacricket.lk/news/player-contract-payments-office-bearers-met-with-players, 12 March 2014.
[130]Andrew Fernando, 'SL Contracts Decision Likely on Thursday', ESPNcricinfo 12 March 2014,

while Jayawardene announced it via the ICC's Twitter Mirror. This did not go down well with Sanath who felt let down by the statements; he had expected them to discuss their future with him rather than with the media.

'I've been very transparent with them. If they're even resting, I've been calling them and telling them what's going on. I never ever dealt controversially with any senior player. When I became a selector, there were a lot of stories and comments in the media, that we were going to do this and that, but we didn't do anything of that sort. I've always handled the seniors in a different way. Whatever respect should be given to that senior player has been given, as a selection panel,' he said.[131]

In a few other interviews, Sanath even labelled the actions of the seniors as 'highly unethical'. 'They should have had the common decency to inform the selectors who could then prepare Sri Lanka for the next phase,' he said in an interview to *Daily Mirror*. 'Traditionally, any international player takes an important decision such as retirement after consulting the selectors first. This shows they are ungrateful for what they got through playing for the country.'[132]

Despite these continued off-field problems, Sri Lanka was progressing well in the tournament as the team made it seamlessly to the finals of the World Twenty20. Sanath, who happened to be in Bangladesh at the time, reconciled with Jayawardene and Sangakkara just before the knockout stages.

'I had a very good chat with Sanga and Mahela. There was a

[131]'Sri Lanka Chief Selector Jayasuriya Feels Let Down by Sangakkara and ESPNcricinfo', *Hindustan Times*, 20 March 2014.
[132]Andrew Fernando, 'I Feel Very Let Down: Jayasuriya', ESPNcircinfo, 18 March 2014.

small miscommunication from their part also, but nothing like that will happen again,' he said. 'They have never had any problems with the selection committee, and they had always wanted to be in touch with me. But after this, we had a very good talk.'[133]

Sri Lanka went on to win the World Twenty20, beating India in the final by 6 wickets. So, in many ways, it was the perfecting ending to Jayawardene and Sangakkara's Twenty20 careers.

The heady heights of the triumph were spoilt by the news that the Head Coach Paul Farbrace was going to jump ship. It had been just three months into the role and Farbrace was being courted by ECB. Sanath did not like the fact that Farbrace, who had been handed the responsibility of designing the transition process, was prepared to leave so soon.

Eventually, Farbrace did quit, leaving Sri Lanka in a state of flux. Sanath's long-term teammate and opening partner Marvan Atapattu stepped in as a stand-in coach for the upcoming England tour, but a permanent solution was still awaited. Sanath, Head of Coaching Jerome Jayaratne and Cricket Committee Chairman Ranjit Fernando were part of a three-man team that recommended Atapattu as the interim head coach.

But Sanath was clearly not amused with Farbrace as he vented his anger in an interview to BBC Sinhala. He refused to blame SLC for exit, but, instead, sympathized with them, calling Farbrace's exit the 'biggest disappointment of his tenure'.

Sanath continued to negotiate with the players as part of a new three-man committee along with Treasurer Nuski Mohammed and CEO Ashley de Silva, for the player contracts. The committee

---

[133]Andrew Fernando, 'Jayasuriya Reconciles with Senior Players', ESPNcricinfo, 25 March 2014.

successfully managed to negotiate a settlement with the players whereby the latter agreed to lower their demands and agreed to settle for a 10 per cent share from the ICC and ACC events. The players finally signed the annual contracts.

With the problem of payments solved, the focus shifted to the English tour. There was this sticky issue of two key players, Malinga and Perera, being away for the IPL. But Sanath was willing to let them continue playing in the cash-rich league.

However, Sanath was not in favour of young Sri Lankan players playing in the IPL as he felt that that would be detrimental to their individual games. Having himself been part of the IPL in its initial years, Sanath's stand surprised many.

But despite these problems, Sri Lanka had one of the most successful tours of England and Ireland, winning all the series at stake in all three formats, including the Test series, capping a memorable first half of 2014.

Meanwhile, in the midst of these pressing matters, Sanath suffered his first real health scare. He had to be treated for a heart ailment at Colombo's famous Nawaloka Hospital. He underwent an angioplasty to install a stent in one of his coronary arteries to clear a blockade. He was advised a long period to recover from his ailment. So, it was hardly a surprise that he opted out of being on the panel to select the next full-time coach for the Sri Lankan side, for which Atapattu was confirmed in a full-time role.

Trouble Brewing

This was also the season when the buildup towards the mega prize in cricket—the World Cup 2015—began in all earnest for Sri Lanka. But a hurriedly arranged India tour for a five-match ODI series spoilt all plans. Senior pros, Jayawardene and Sangakkara, were once again vocal in their criticism as the tour went pear-shaped. Sri Lanka lost the series by 0-5, but not before all sorts of issues came to the fore.

Sanath felt that the senior pros were making comments that revealed Sri Lanka's plans. Jayawardene mentioned that he was keen to open, while Sangakkara was 'disappointed' at being sent home midway through the series. Sanath now wanted to leave Jayawardene and Sangakkara completely out of the selection discussions.

'By the way things are happening, we might even have to keep them out of the meetings where plans are discussed,' he told *Daily Mirror*. 'This is setting a dangerous precedent. What they have told media are things that we had discussed at a meeting. They were just basic ideas only. Nothing was final. When they go and tell the media as if it were all their plans, it puts us in an embarrassing situation.'[134]

Sanath criticized Sangakkara in particular. 'Those are decisions that the national selectors should take, not the players,' he said. 'If the players are going to do our job, what is the point of having selectors there at all? I had a one-to-one chat with Sanga and he did not protest the decision at all.'[135]

Sri Lanka somehow recovered in the buildup, beating a hapless English side by 5-2 at home, before heading to New Zealand for a pre-World Cup series. This proved to be a nightmare tour as Sri Lanka went down by 2-4 in a seven-match series. Sanath was

---

[134]Channaka De Silva, 'Jayasuriya Miffed at Seniors Spilling Beans', *Daily Mirror*, 13 November 2014.
[135]Andrew Fernando, 'Player Comments Upset Jayasuriya', ESPNcricinfo, 13 November 2014.

clearly alarmed by the results in New Zealand, as he pressed the panic button. All the gains of 2014 had been frittered away and it all came to a head during the showpiece event.

Sri Lanka's loss in the quarter-final of the ICC Cricket World Cup 2015 to South Africa proved to be the final straw. Sanath received a lot of criticism. Then, politics as usual played a part with an interim committee appointed to run SLC, till the next administration was elected. That put Sanath's future as chief selector in doubt. The interim committee, now headed by Sidath Wettimuny, a former Test batsman, had dropped enough hints about Sanath not getting an extension.

The comments made by Minister of Sports Navin Dissanayake and Wettimuny, after the loss to South Africa, forced the hand of Sanath's panel.

'There were issues with selection all round. I wouldn't agree with some of the selections that happened,' Dissanayake said. 'You cannot come to a conclusion where Sri Lanka cricket is from one match against South Africa. But I have been critical of the selection process and some of the things that have happened. I don't want it to happen in the future, that's why I appointed a professional interim committee.'[136]

Wettimuny said it was important to have fresh thinking during the selection. 'If the same bunch looks at the same crop of players all the time, I don't think that's good,' Wettimuny said.[137]

Sanath read the writing on the wall. He opted to resign and

[136]Sa'adi Thawfeeq, 'Jayasuriya-led Selection Panel Quits', ESPNcricinfo, 3 April 2015.
[137]Sa'adi Thawfeeq, 'Jayasuriya-led Selection Panel Quits', ESPNcricinfo, 3 April 2015.

sent in a letter to Minister of Sports Navin Dissanayake, citing the possible end of his tenure as the head of the selection committee as the reason. Not just Sanath, his fellow selectors also resigned, sending separate letters of resignation.

In his email to Dissanayake, Jayasuriya stated, 'I am extremely proud and happy that during my tenure, Sri Lanka was able to emerge world champions in T20, win the Asia Cup and a long-awaited Test series against England as well and also emerge semi-finalists in the Champions Trophy. These are milestones the Sri Lanka cricket team, including the entire selection committee and coaching staff, worked extremely hard for. These are achievements that we can be proud of as Sri Lankans.'[138]

Added to the selection panel's exit, Sri Lanka was also losing its greats like Jayawardene and Sangakkara to retirement. So yet again, Sri Lanka was in a state of clutter, this time of its own making. For Sanath, all the responsibilities of the past twelve months were gone. He was no longer a minister or MP. But in Sri Lankan cricket, you can never say a final goodbye to anyone.

Yet Another Comeback

Sanath's erstwhile cabinet colleague and businessman, Thilanga Sumathipala, returned as president of SLC. So, there was widespread speculation about Sanath's return as well.

And it happened!

Sanath made a dramatic return as chief selector in just twelve months after stepping down voluntarily. This time, he was to be in the company of his former teammate Romesh Kaluwitharna and

---

[138]Ibid.

off-spinner Ranjith Madurasingha, apart from a colleague from his previous stint, Upashantha. Sanath was to replace former Captain Aravinda de Silva as the chairman of selectors.

'I took this job on because I like the challenge,' he said. 'Thilanga (Sumathipala) and the sports minister had a lot of confidence in me. They knew what I did during my first two-year stint as chief selector. Thilanga has been in touch with me from the first day he was elected SLC president. He asked me what kind of a role I can play to help Sri Lanka cricket, he knows how hard I work and my commitment.'[139]

When taking over, Sanath announced that his new panel would have to 'start from the bottom', because his predecessors had set the team back. Sri Lanka had regressed as a side from the time Sanath had left in April 2015, winning just once against a full-member Test playing side.

'I did everything 100 per cent for Sri Lankan cricket. First we need to look at which players had been chosen in the past,' he told BBC Sinhala. 'Sometimes you pick young players and then later, these players are dropped and fresh players are brought in. When fresh players are brought in, it takes them a while to succeed, and the players you had been investing in are ignored. That is what happened there.'[140]

But the second stint was anything but rosy. There were problems galore. And it started with losses in England, followed by drubbing in South Africa. The saving grace was a clean sweep

[139]Sa'adi Thawfeeq, 'We Have the Top Bowling Side in the World', ESPNcricinfo, 8 May 2016.
[140]Andrew Fernando, 'Selectors will Have to Start from the Bottom: Jayasuriya', ESPNcricinfo, 3 May 2016.

162

in a Test against Australia at home, apart from Twenty20 series wins in South Africa and Australia.

There were other problems, for example, with regard to the leadership of the side. Mathews kept getting injured. As a result, Upul Tharanga, Rangana Herath and Chandimal wore the hats of leadership at various times in several formats. Chandimal lost his place in the limited-overs squad and Sanath advised him to go back to his roots.

'Chandimal should go back to club cricket,' he told Cricbuzz. 'He should work his game out. This is not the first time he has gone through a tough patch. He has to be mentally very strong. You can't think of failure all the time. Have a chat with the computer analyst, find out what's going wrong and come back stronger. These are tough times for him. You find media and social media going after you, and you have to keep these things aside and concentrate on your cricket.'[141]

But this was a bone of contention with Sanath's former teammates and they lashed out at him for his approach with Chandimal. First off the block was his ex-captain Arjuna Ranatunga. 'I am bitterly disappointed with what these people have done with Chandimal. They have destroyed him,' Ranatunga told *The Island*.[142]

Another former captain, Sangakkara, lashed out saying that the selectors had missed the plot completely. 'We've had two, two-and-a-half years of it now, looking for replacements for (Tillakaratne) Dilshan, Mahela (Jayawardene). One man that was identified very

---

[141]Rex Clementine, 'Jayasuriya Promises South Africa Taste of their Own Medicine', 11 February 2017.
[142]Rex Clementine, 'Stop Harassing Chandimal', says Arjuna', *The Island*, 5 July 2017.

early was Dinesh Chandimal, who performed excellently in South Africa, then in England, in Australia. He's actually had a period where he's been identified as the best young player (and was) appointed captain probably a bit too soon. Then he was dropped from the captaincy, dropped from the team, so he's never had a consistent run in the position that he was identified for,' he said.[143]

The Final Straw

Sanath's personal life was added to the mix as a sex tape with former partner Maleeka Sirisena was leaked. This meant that even as Sri Lanka struggled to stay afloat in the ICC Champions Trophy in 2017, questions about his future as a selector arose.

'Recently his private life video is leaked to the media and it is very bad public perception and we don't want him to continue as a selector. He has disgraced the game and the nation,' one of the top SLC board officials was quoted as saying from Colombo in the *Deccan Chronicle*.[144]

There was criticism about making as many as 38 players playing in 30 ODIs in one year since Sanath had taken over again. The team had won just nine of those games, losing 17. But despite these allegations, Sanath's panel was given a six-month extension by the Minister of Sports Dayasiri Jayasekera.

Interference of the SLC President Sumathipala was also a constant irritant. Graham Ford had returned as head coach, but

---

[143]'Hunt for Veterans' Replacement Went Too Long for Sri Lanka: Kumar Sangarakka', *The Indian Express*, 27 December 2018.
[144]Bipin Dani, 'Sanath Jayasuriya's Future as Sri Lanka Selector in Jeopardy after Leaked Sex Video?', *Deccan Chronicle*, 31 May 2017.

constant losses along with controversial selections, like left-arm spinner Sachith Pathirana, forced him to quit. There were allegations that Pathirana's father was a friend of Sumathipala's and controlled votes in SLC. His selection also led to more criticism for Sanath.

Cricket writer Rex Clementine did not hold back his punches in this piece he wrote for *The Island*:[145]

> Currently the national cricket team is like the National List of the Parliament. The National List is meant to bring in country's highly educated and resourced persons into Parliament. Luminaries like Lakshman Kadirgamar and Professor G.L. Pieris made their parliament debuts through the National List. But in modern day politics, the National List is meant for political rejects. Similarly, although the national cricket team is meant for the best talented, at the moment we see people entertaining their whims and fancies. Otherwise, how on earth can we use 45 players in two years in ODI cricket. The only reason why Sachith Pathirana has featured regularly in the national team in recent times is because his father has control over six votes at the cricket AGM. Other talented left-arm spinners like Malinda Pushpakumara and Amila Aponso are left in the lurch.
>
> So, Ford is not the only person to be blamed for Sri Lanka's disappointing run in recent times. SLC Chief Thilanga Sumathipala and Chairman of Selectors Sanath Jayasuriya are equally responsbile. If they have any self-respect given Sri Lanka's steady decline in the last two years, both of them should do a Ford and resign from their positions.

---

[145]Rex Clementine, 'Shame on Sri Lanka's Cricket: Arjuna', *The Island*, 9 September 2013.

Ford left the side in a state of disarray that was best signified by the 2-3 ODI series loss to Zimbabwe at home. What really broke the back of the camel was a humiliating series defeat at the hands of India in August–September 2017. Sri Lanka was whitewashed by 0-3 in the Tests and lost the first three ODIs, forcing Sanath's panel to quit en masse. This was just two months after they had been given a six-month extension. There were still two more ODIs and a Twenty20 International left in the India tour. The panel had already named squads for the same.

Sanath and his panel sent a combined letter bearing the names of his panellists to the Minister of Sports Jayasekara.

The letter sent out on 29 August 2017 has been reproduced below:[146]

Dear Sir,

I write this letter with great sadness in my heart as after long discussion with fellow selectors, we have unanimously decided to tender our resignation on 7 September 2017.

as a player who has represented the country at all levels, and as a former captain and current chairman of selectors, last Sunday's incident at the grounds was the last straw. Cricket has been and will always be my life, so it was particularly painful to see our own fans attack our own players.

I acknowledge it has been a very disappointing year. However, just one year ago we beat Australia at home 3-0. This was an unforgettable moment. We have some very talented boys and I am sure in time they will take cricket to

---

[146]'Jayasuriya's Resgination Letter to Sri Lanka Minister of Sports', ESPNcricinfo, 30 August 2017.

the heights that it once was. We will always be ready to help Sri Lanka cricket should the need arise.

The 1996 players always will think of the glory days with nostalgia. We would like to thank you, sir, for all the help and support extended to us. We would also like to thank the president and the board for the unwavering support that was extended to us.

Finally, we would like to thank the team for giving us their best at all times. We go with our eyes full of tears but with our heads held high. To all the fans we say please have faith in the boys. They will deliver. To the boys, we say: believe in your ability and believe in the fans. They will be with you ultimately. We believe we will keep to our vision and succeed as one team, one nation.

Yours faithfully,
Sanath Jayasuriya

Thus, Sanath's two stints as chairman of selectors ended, but you never know when he makes a return if the stars align once again!

8
—

Shaking More Than a
Leg in India

Mumbai and Colombo are similar in a number of ways. Both are coastal cities, have beaches galore and the lifestyle of the inhabitants is very much 'live and let live'. Therefore, most Sri Lankans feel at home in Mumbai. Sanath, too, had a liking for the city. In his playing days, he did not spend much time in Mumbai, but still developed an affinity towards it—perhaps because of his performance as well.

'Mumbai is a city very special to me; I have lots of friends (there),' he said in an interview in his later years.[147]

He scored 87 in the only Test he played at the Wankhede

[147]'Mumbai is a City Very Special to Me', http://life.dailymirror.lk/article/63/celebrities/1975/qmumbai-is-a-city-very-special-to-meq-sanath-jayasuriya, 14 July 2012.

Stadium in 1997 on his first full tour to India under Arjuna Ranatunga. He scored a 50 in the first innings and followed it up with 37 in the second. He also picked up two crucial wickets with his left-arm spin, that of Navjot Sidhu and the then India captain, Sachin Tendulkar, just as they were looking to score.

That very year, in the month of May in 1997, Sanath owned Wankhede Stadium once again when he spoilt India's celebration of their 50th year of independence. He yet again smashed hapless Indian bowlers to all corners of the stadium and ended with a whopping unbeaten 151 off just 120 balls with 17 boundaries and 4 sixes.

This was then the highest individual score in ODI cricket by a Sri Lankan, snatching the record away from teammate Aravinda de Silva. It was incidentally also the same time when Sanath held the record for the best batting and bowling figures in ODIs for a Sri Lankan. His figures of 6 for 29 against England in 1992–93 was still the best then.

Therefore, for him, it was an easy call to accept a chance to spend time in Mumbai.

Million-dollar Baby is Here

In September 2007, when the BCCI launched its multi-million dollar Twenty20 IPL, Sanath was expected to fetch a huge price. For the first time, private owners were going to own teams and would have the ability to buy any player from any corner of the world as part of their squads. It was the first example of open market policy being applied to a cricket event. Some of India's biggest businessmen and top Bollywood actors and actresses were going to enter the field of cricket for the first time as team owners.

So a dash of glamour and panache was going to be institutionalized in cricket forever.

The Fab Four of Indian cricket—Sachin Tendulkar (Mumbai), Rahul Dravid (Bengaluru), Sourav Ganguly (Kolkata) and V.V.S. Laxman (Hyderabad)—had already been allocated teams even before the auction. They were nominated as the icons for their respective franchise. Laxman later recused himself from that position, but his presence as an unnamed icon was never in doubt.

On 20 February 2008, when the IPL conducted its first-ever player auction at the Trident hotel in Mumbai's busy Nariman Point, it was meant to be the start of a new era for players in terms of their salaries. Players were going to be bought at an auction with owners vying with themselves to buy their favourites.

Sanath was expected to go at a healthy sum because he had pegged himself at US$250,000. His name came under the hammer of noted auctioneer Richard Madley in the second round. The first round of auction had seen the likes of India's latest icon Mahendra Singh Dhoni, Adam Gilchrist, Sanath's countrymen Muttiah Muralitharan and Mahela Jayawardene, Australian spin wizard Shane Warne and the Rawalpindi Express and Shoaib Akhtar, being snapped up various by franchises. Dhoni topped the earnings at that stage with his price tag of US$1.5 million from Chennai Super Kings.

Then the second round of the auction began. First up was India's then Test captain Anil Kumble, who doubled his base price of US$250,000 as he was picked by Royal Challengers Bangalore. It was the turn of Kumble's spin twin Harbhajan Singh to be picked up next. Harbhajan also came at a base price of US$250,000 but he ultimately went for US$850,000 to the Mukesh Ambani-owned Mumbai Indians.

When Sanath's name was pulled out next, there was an immediate buzz in the room. Teams had quick confabulations but it was Mumbai Indians who were again quick off the blocks. They had made up their mind to go for Sanath and finally bought him at a price of US$975,000. This was a massive jump for Sanath, but it also underlined his value in the shortest format, at least in the eyes of those willing to pay the big bucks.

Sanath was the highest bid player in the second round of the auction, beating even the likes of Kumar Sangakkara who came under the hammer right after him. 'I know my cost is big news. But I know the price has come owing to my contribution to the national team over the years. Now, it is my responsibility to ensure that the Mumbai team benefits worthily for the money they are spending on me,' Sanath said in his first reaction after the auction.[148]

Tendulkar was to be Sanath's captain and also possibly his opening partner. The two had sparred a lot against each other through the 1990s. But they never had an opportunity to bat together, except once. However, both had featured in a charity match for the Princess Diana Fund at Lord's in 1998.

So there was an air of excitement about this partnership that was unique in many ways. Both were entertainers, but had their own unique ways of doing so. While Sanath bludgeoned his way to sixes, Tendulkar sometimes killed them softly.

Interestingly, Sanath was in Australia with the Sri Lankan squad to take part in a tri-series, which also featured India, apart from the host. In fact, both Tendulkar and Sanath were in Australia when

---

[148]'It's a Dream Come True to Play With Sachin: Jayasuriya', https://www.dnaindia.com/sports/report-it-s-a-dream-come-true-to-play-with-sachin-jayasuriya-1153532

the auction made headlines all over the world, and so, Sanath had a chance to discuss with Tendulkar the plans for their new side and their brand new association. 'I met up with him in Hobart during the one-day series in Australia and discussed the IPL. It will be a great thing in my career to open with Sachin (Tendulkar), the best player in the world. I am really happy to open with him. I will give my best for Mumbai,' said Sanath in an interview.

While the news of Sanath earning the mega bucks in the first edition of IPL was spreading, there was some bad news coming as well. SLC virtually shut the door on his international career by dropping him from the list of contracted players for 2008–09. Sri Lankan newspaper *Daily Mirror* quoted selection committee sources as saying that they had 'decided to drop the veteran all-rounder from a list of players to be contracted for next year'.

He had already been dropped for the West Indies tour due to poor form. 'Jayasuriya will only be offered tour contracts if he is selected,' selection committee sources said. 'Only four "A" grade players such as Mahela Jayawardene, Kumar Sangakkara, Muttiah Muralitharan and Chaminda Vaas have been picked for next year,' sources told the *Daily Mirror*.[149]

The man in charge of deciding Sanath's fate was none other than his own first captain Arjuna Ranatunga. The well-built former captain was now the president of SLC and responsible for deciding these matters. Ranatunga headed an interim committee that ran the SLC and, hence, had the final authority on such matters. 'We will offer the player contracts after the interim committee approves the

[149]'Sri Lanka Board Drops Jayasuriya from Contract List', https://www.dnaindia.com/sports/report-sri-lanka-board-drops-jayasuriya-from-contract-list-1159477

list. There are a few issues still to be discussed, such as the amount of money offered for each contract category and the composition of players in each category,' SLC chief executive officer Duleep Mendis told *Daily Mirror*.[150]

Meanwhile, Sanath got engaged with all the buildup to the IPL. He was present at a photocall for the launch of Mumbai Indians. The focus remained the partnership of Sanath and Tendulkar. But Sanath was keen to point at other players within the squad, for example, the recently retired South African all-rounder Shaun Pollock, compatriot Dilhara Fernando and young Indian batsman Robin Uthappa.

'It (Twenty20) may be a young man's game but I have worked hard. I will try and make sure Mumbai wins (the title). I am young too. I am very fit and working hard. I want to perform with bat and ball,' announced Sanath.[151]

The Mumbai Indians squad itself was well-balanced, with a number of experienced players joining forces with Mumbai Ranji players like Ajinkya Rahane, Abhishek Nayar, Dhawal Kulkarni and (now disgraced) Aniket Chavan. Nearly six years later, Chavan along with former Indian fast bowler Sreesanth and off-spinner Ajit Chandila were to be the poster boys of what went wrong with the IPL over the years. They were alleged to have been part of a large spot-fixing racket that engulfed the tournament and thereafter changed the way the sport was run forever in India.

The tournament started with much fanfare, but in the Mumbai Indians camp, there were many worries. Tendulkar could not start

---

[150]IANS, 'Sri Lanka Board Drops Jayasuriya from Contract List', DNA, 11 April 2008.
[151]'Jayasuriya Hoping to Impress in IPL', rediff.com, 9 April 2008.

the tournament because of an injury and there was an interim skipper in the form of Harbhajan. The team struggled to get going and lost the first four games.

But Sanath did make a mark. So fierce were Sanath's upper cuts in the first match of the season against Royal Challengers Bangalore that it broke the nose of a hapless sports photographer, Andrea Fernandes, who was doing her first assignment ever! Andrea was admitted to the nearby Harkishandas Hospital in Charni Road, with a fractured nose. 'Wow...it was Jayasuriya! I wasn't aware who the batsman was but I am thankful it wasn't a six. If a four can break my nose, imagine what a six would have done,' she said.[152]

Fernandes has now been a photographer for more than three years but she still cannot forget her first assignment because of Sanath. 'From this experience I have learnt that safety is needed no matter where you are,' she said.[153]

Flawed Campaign

In between, there was another setback when Harbhajan got into an ugly brawl with Kings XI fast bowler Sreesanth. Harbhajan slapped Sreesanth and faced sanctions from BCCI and match-referee Farokh Engineer. As a result, after a protracted battle, Harbhajan was immediately banned from the rest of the tournament.

Now Mumbai Indians were facing a real quandary. Harbhajan was banned and Tendulkar was still injured. They had no idea whom to turn to. The squad had two veterans and former national captains in Sanath and Pollock. But both were reluctant to take up

---

[152]Sanath Jayasuriya blogspot, 22 April 2008.
[153]Ibid.

the jobs. Finally, the team management convinced Pollock to do the role, freeing Sanath to play the senior statesman's role.

That really did the trick as Sanath flourished in this new role of a senior statesman. His initial scores were 29, 20, 1. With Pollock in charge, he flourished with the ball when he fetched a Man of the Match award in Kolkata for his spell of 3 for 14. This was also incidentally Mumbai Indians' first win after four losses.

Thereafter, Sanath's bat started doing the talking. It really came to the fore in the 8th match of the season against Chennai Super Kings, and that too, at home. Just before the game, Sanath had to rush to Sri Lanka for a couple of days for some personal work. This break did wonders.

'In the first three games, I was getting out for 20s and 30s. That was worrying as that had been the case in the last four or five months for me,' recalled Sanath. This was also the match that marked the return of Tendulkar from his injury break. The famed partnership of Sanath and Tendulkar was also going to be unveiled for the first time in the tournament. The match was a first for many reasons for the IPL. It was the first time Tendulkar was to play in the tournament. So it was an occasion to remember for all. But it was Sanath who made it memorable as he smashed an unbeaten 48-ball 114 with 11 boundaries and 9 sixes. Tendulkar, at the other end, could only applaud as the Matara Mauler went berserk. 'When I went back to Mumbai after a brief break, my rhythm was back,' he said.[154]

Mumbai Indians were now on a roll, winning five matches on the trot thanks mainly to Sanath's bat. He had scores of 48, 36, 20,

---

[154]Rex Clementine, 'Sanath on IPL, Sachin, Money in Cricket and Test Matches', The Island, http://www.island.lk/2008/06/15/sports4.html

66, 38 and 54 to keep Mumbai in the hunt. It came to the point that Mumbai needed just two more wins to make it to the play-offs. But that was not to be. Mumbai Indians' campaign, which started as a nightmare, picked up as a dream but ultimately ended in a narrow crash.

However, the Tendulkar-Sanath partnership did live up to the preseason hype. 'People were thrilled to see both of us opening. I have always enjoyed Sachin's company and we had mutual respect as opponents and playing in the same team was an unbelievable experience,' Sanath explained later in an interview.[155]

'When I was going after the bowling, Sachin would come to me and remind that we had scored enough runs and now's the time to completely demoralize the opposition and not to lose my wicket. He comes up with various suggestions as well. He's a very simple and a nice man. He's also a good team player and gives confidence to youngsters and I think a lot of younger players learnt from him.'[156]

Mumbai Indians finished fifth, a creditable finish considering the troubles they had off the field. But Sanath blamed himself partly for letting the team down at crucial stages. 'We lost three very close games in the last over. I am responsible for losing one game along with Dilhara. But other than that, there was no luck going for us at all, but overall, we played good cricket as we came from behind to beat stronger teams,' rued Sanath.[157]

Despite his modest assessment, Sanath was an unqualified success story for Mumbai Indians. He topped the batting charts

[155]Ibid.
[156]Ibid.
[157]Ibid.

for the side with 514 runs from 14 games at a strike rate of 166.34 with one century and two half-centuries.

'I enjoyed the IPL. Apart from the cricket I played, I had the opportunity of meeting some guys who had been my fierce opponents over the years. You learn other cultures and get to know some of these players too. The Reliance Group, the owner of Mumbai Indians, was very good to us as well. Mr Mukesh Ambani was firmly behind us and treated us well. When we were losing the first few games, they didn't put any pressure. They basically treated us like their own family,' recalled Sanath.[158]

That family-like feeling was reciprocated some 10 years later, when Sanath was duly remembered and called to celebrate the 10th-year anniversary of Mumbai Indians in 2017. In fact, not just Sanath, but every member or support staff of the Mumbai Indians squad over a decade was part of the celebrations.

Not So Young Anymore

By the time the second edition of the IPL was to start, Sanath had already touched the cricketing ripe old age of forty! That became the focus of all attention as questions surrounding his age began being asked. Of course the fact that the IPL itself had to be uprooted and moved to South Africa due to Indian General Elections did not matter, or the fact that there were a number of veterans in the tournament.

Mumbai Indians employed a new fitness trainer Ramji Srinivasan and he was asked about the mix of old and young in his squad. At that stage, T20 cricket was considered a young man's

---

[158]Ibid.

game, but over the years, the perception has changed.

'We are not here to make Sanath run like a twenty-year-old. Each player has his own strength and weakness. My job is see to that a player develops core strength depending on his discipline and importantly focus on injury prevention,' remarked Ramji.[159]

But forty or not forty, Sanath's enthusiasm on the field soon became the topic of discussion. His fielding and fitness was still remarkable so it became all the more reason for everyone to sit up and take notice. The team owner Nita Ambani, for one, was an instant fan.

'When I watch Sanath Jayasuriya on the field, I find him so agile that he can put a twenty-year-old to shame. I can't believe that he is forty,' said Nita Ambani after the team's win against Chennai Super Kings in the first match of the 2009 season.[160]

Sanath was also an inspiration for some of his younger teammates like J.P. Duminy and Shikhar Dhawan. So overall, this new-found role of inspiring everyone around him was quite different from the first edition of IPL where Sanath had to do all the running for his side. Before the tournament started, Sanath also held the record for the most sixes (31) in the IPL until that stage. Sanath had also hit more boundaries, 57, than anyone else at that stage. No wonder then that Sanath was the highest insured amongst the overseas players before the tournament got underway in South Africa.

---

[159]'Indian Trainers No Way Inferior: Ramji', *The New Indian Express*, 27 December 2018.
[160]'I Can't Believe Jayasuriya is 40', Sanath Jayasuriya Blogspot, http://sanath189.blogspot.com/2009/04/i-cant-believe-jayasuriya-is-40-nita.html, 24 April 2009.

The second IPL season had been insured for a total of US$286 million, more than double that of the $125-million cover in 2008, and included provisions for acts of terrorism and cancelled matches. It also included ten-fold increases, in some cases, in individual covers to be provided by Oriental Insurance Corporation (OIC).

Dhoni attracted the highest individual insurance cover of US$10.5 million, while Sanath was the highest insured among overseas players, for around US$6 million. The package took into account all the 120 auctioned players. The cost in premiums to the franchises was around US$430,000 each. No wonder then that the 2009 edition of IPL was one where Sanath's performance was scrutinized a lot. But he was ready for it, as he himself admitted during the course of the tournament.

'As you get older in cricket, your performance gets scrutinized more because there are a lot of youngsters pushing for your place. One has to keep performing and the margin of error gets reduced with time,' he noted. However, he was quick to stress that there is no substitute for experience. 'But every team needs experience; there's no alternative for it, and many teams have realized that.'[161]

Sanath and his skipper Tendulkar put up a spectacular show when they went hammer and tongs at the Kolkata Knight Riders bowlers. So much so that even bipartisan watchers were forced to gush in awe.

'It's a rare treat for us...we are not going to see this every day,' quipped a South African journalist as Tendulkar and Sanath went beserk at Port Elizabeth's St. George's Park with a flurry of boundaries and sixes. Sanath smashed his first half-century (52) of

---

[161]G.S. Vivek, 'No Alternative to Experience', Journalism of Courage Archive, 19 April 2009.

the second edition of IPL. But Mumbai continued to make a few mistakes and the going was tougher in 2009 than in 2008. That famous turnaround of 2008 was nowhere to be seen.

Sanath put that down to closely matched teams in the 2009 teams. 'Because teams are more closely matched in this tournament, we are seeing tighter matches and more cliffhangers than in the inaugural IPL. This means that the teams that cope best under pressure will take more of the 50/50 matches,' he wrote in his syndicated column.[162]

The inconsistent batting of Mumbai Indians was the major cause for concern. Sanath, too, had disappointing returns as he logged just one more half-century and was then dropped for the first time from the Mumbai Indians XI. He was dropped for the game against Delhi Daredevils, but skipper Tendulkar had an apologetic explanation for the same. 'It wasn't easy but those are the calls that you've got to take from time to time. Shaun (Pollock, head coach) and me went up to him (Sanath) and said that he had to sit out this game and he accepted that,' Tendulkar explained during the toss.[163]

Back in Mumbai, ex-Mumbai Indians' coach, Lalchand Rajput, was one of the first ones to be critical of the move. Having closely watched Sanath's destructive abilities in 2008, he was surprised by the move to drop Sanath. As the campaign went into a tailspin, Sanath once again took to his syndicated column to offer support to his beleaguered side. 'For us, the key will be more batting support

---

[162]Sanath Jayasuriya, 'Challengers Responding Well to Kumble's Leadership', http://www.sify.com/sports/challengers-responding-well-to-kumble-s-leadership-news-columns-jfdme1giahfsi.html, 12 May 2009.
[163]Toss interview video clip.

for JP (Duminy). He has been the cornerstone of our batting but the rest of the top and middle order have not provided sufficient backup. Some of that responsibility will fall on me and I feel ready to rise to that challenge. The management went for a new strategy on Friday night and left me out. As a player, that was disappointing.'[164]

The anguish and the criticisms had the salutary effect as the axe lasted for just one game. The results, however, continued to dry up. Mumbai Indians' campaign finally ended on a whimper as they finished seventh in an eight-team competition, definitely causing a lot of heartburn in the camp.

End of an Association

A lot had changed by the time Sanath returned for the third edition of IPL. He had been dropped by Sri Lanka even from their ODI squad and it was likely that his career would come to a halt. In the midst of all this, Sanath had announced that he was joining active politics. He was to contest from his beloved hometown of Matara.

Just a day before he left for India to be part of the IPL, Sanath cast his vote. Sanath cast his vote at the Matara District Secretary's office. Under Clause 20C of the Parliamentary Elections Act, the vote would be considered a postal vote. This created a lot of flutter back home in Sri Lanka, but by the time he landed in Mumbai, his focus was completely on the tournament. He had been the torchbearer of Mumbai Indians' performances in 2008, but in 2009, he had slightly disappointed with the bat. So the pressure

---

[164]Sanath Jayasuriya, 'Key to Mumbai's Success is More Batting Support to Duminy', http://www.sify.com/sports/key-to-mumbai-s-success-is-more-batting-support-to-duminy-news-columns-jflmD7ihahcsi.html, 12 May 2009.

was telling. Midway through the tournament, the news that Sanath had won a place in the Sri Lankan parliament added a different dimension to his personality.

This time, however, Sanath was not the same on the field. His first three games saw poor returns of 23, 7 and 2. There was verbal support from the head coach Robin Singh.

'Sanath is a seasoned cricketer and he knows what is best for him. It is a question of getting him motivated to play his role,' Robin told reporters ahead of the fourth match against Kolkata Knight Riders.[165]

But those words hardly mattered as Sanath was dropped from the playing XI for the second time in his IPL career. On the sidelines, Sanath kept praising his squad in his syndicated columns. 'There is so much talent in this Mumbai Indians team and we need to trust ourselves, and each other, to perform. One other reason we have to be confident is our team spirit and unity. Unlike some franchises who have struggled to gel this season, we are like a family.'

But unfortunately, Sanath's wait kept getting longer and longer. He got just one more game and he was never in the reckoning. By the time play-offs came along, Sanath had important duties back home. He had to be sworn in to the parliament. He took off just before the finals against Chennai Super Kings, was sworn in as a member of parliament, and was back in Mumbai. However, he could only watch the finals from the sidelines as Mumbai Indians ended up in a runner-up position.

For two years, Mumbai Indians faced a struggle to put together a side to challenge the best in the IPL. It was ironic that the man

---

[165]'Sanath Knows What is Good For Him: Robin Singh', *The Times of India*, 21 March 2010.

who had held them together for the better part of two years was left out when they eventually got into a roll in 2010.

The squad did, however, qualify to play in the now defunct domestic champions' clash called Champions League Twenty20. The tournament held in September 2010 was staged in South Africa, but there was a big disappointment in store as Sanath was left out of the squad completely.

Therefore, it was hardly a surprise that when IPL announced fresh auctions for the 2011 edition, Sanath went unsold. None of the other franchises, apart from Mumbai Indians, bid for him. His waning form coupled with his age made him a complete no-go. But Sanath took the omission sportingly.

'I am not disappointed and have no complaints. I was associated with the team for three years and have good memories. They are a fantastic side and Sachin is leading the team brilliantly. I wish them good luck,' Sanath said to *The Times of India*.[166]

He did, however, make a trip to his favourite city of Mumbai during the 2011 IPL, but to the studio of the host broadcaster, SET Max. Interestingly, it was during this trip that Sanath gave an indication of what could be in store for him next in Mumbai.

During one of the pregame show, Sanath, in a bid to show some support to the dipping fortunes of Adam Gilchrist-led Kings XI Punjab, announced that he would dance if they won. Almost on cue, Gilchrist heard that and mentioned it in his celebratory post-match presentation interview.

Always a sport, Sanath kept his promise and did a small jig.

---

[166]Krishna Kanta Chakraborty, 'I Will Miss the MI Dressing Room: Jayasuriya', *The Times of India*, 11 January 2011.

More Than Just a Jig

Little did he know that the jig would get him back to Mumbai a year later, not for cricket, but for a completely new ball game. He was going to appear in the Indian version of *Dancing with the Stars—Jhalak Dikhhla Jaa*.

This was going to be the 5th season of the reality show. It featured three very high profile judges. Leading the pack was Bollywood's female superstar Madhuri Dixit, who was finding her way back into the tinsel town, leading film-maker Karan Johar, and top choreographer Remo D'Souza. Sanath was paired with a choreographer called Suchitra for the show.

The show usually features a celebrity from any walk of life and a choreographer who trains the contestant. The contest has various challenges. Almost every week, a contestant is eliminated, leading to the grand finale.

'I have never been on a dance field. This is the first time I am doing something like this. But it's a good experience for me,' said Sanath at the launch of the show. 'First, I need to see what kind of dancing I will need to do because we have a culture, we have some kind of a system in our country. We are more conservative people,' he said, adding that his people viewed him as a cricketer. 'Now when I am involved with these things (dancing), they are looking at me differently. So I need to be very careful.'[167]

At the age of forty-two, Sanath was required to groove to Bollywood, salsa, rumba, Latin, contemporary and hip-hop beats

---

[167]'My Legs Move on Pitch, Not Dance Floor: Sanath Jayasuriya', https://archive.mid-day.com/sports/2012/jun/150612-My-legs-move-on-pitch-not-dance-floor:-Sanath-Jayasuriya.htm, 15 June 2012.

with his choreographer. But he was not sure he could match the experts on the dance floor. 'We go out and dance at normal parties. But it's not anything close to the dance taught here. It's totally different. My legs can move on the cricketing field, not for these dance sequences,' he said.[168]

The surprise that Sanath was part of the show was unveiled at a grand launch press conference held in Mumbai. Sanath confirmed that his fears about dancing were indeed right when he hit the dance floor with Madhuri. Both danced to Madhuri's hit number 'Tamma Tamma Loge'.

It was a sight to behold as Madhuri held the fort, while Sanath just stood there pointing a finger here and there. He just could not match Madhuri's brilliance and decided that discretion was the better part of valour. Nevertheless, he won cheers galore from the audience at the launch—a response he hoped regular show viewers would also provide.

Up against Sanath in the show was a wide variety of contestants, especially a group of television and film actors. These included Indian television actors Gurmeet Choudhary, Rashami Desai, Rithvik Dhanjani, Jayati Bhatia, (late) Pratyusha Banerjee, Giaa Manek, and movie actors Isha Sharvani and Ravi Kishan. Also in the fray were female comic star Bharti Singh, anchors Shibani Dandekar and Archana Vijaya, noted ghazal singer Talat Aziz, apart from the then child prodigies Darsheel Safary and Avneet Kaur.

Looking at the field he was up against, Sanath's decision surprised his friends, family and fans when the news of his participation spread.

'My contemporaries are surprised because I am a person of

---

[168]Ibid.

a different kind. And when I say yes to these things, they are a little surprised. They have mixed feelings. So some comments were good, some weren't good, and so I was a bit worried too,' he said.[169]

'I am not nervous. I am just not a good dancer, and so it will take a little time to get into my system. I feel I am stepping into something which is not in my comfort zone. But as a human being, one should try new things. As long as it is not affecting my future career, I am fine with new things,' he added.[170]

When the promo featuring Sanath was unveiled, it featured him in a dressing room receiving a gift from Madhuri. He then breaks into a dance, which yet again confirmed his discomfiture with dancing, though he did sport a smile.

In the very first episode of the show, Indian off-spinner and Sanath's long-term adversary Harbhajan Singh came on to introduce him. Harbhajan did the traditional bhangra to welcome Sanath and even pushed the Sri Lankan legend to dance with him. Sanath for once seemed to be at ease because he had someone he knew accompanying him on the dance floor.

But when the show started, Sanath stunned everyone, especially the judges, with his performance. The very first competitive performance for Sanath was right up his alley as it required him to be in cricketing whites. The dance was based on a cricketing song, which required him to use a bat, helmet and just move. This fitted very well with Sanath. The reactions of the three judges post the dance explained how he had left them amazed. For Remo specifically, it was the case of a hero performing, albeit on a different field.

Madhuri praised him in Sinhalese, saying, '*Gondhak hundai* (Very good)', which instantly made Sanath smile. Then, Madhuri started singing a famous Sinhalese song, '*Surangini, maali, surangini malu...*' and she got Sanath to sing along. Karan Johar, on the other hand, could not stop referring to him as 'sir' and hailed his spirit.

The three judges gave him a standing ovation and he could only react with a sheepish smile. All three gave him 9 points each out of 10, leading him to poll 27 out of the available 30 points. This was a shocking result and catapulted Sanath directly to the top three after the very first competitive performance!

'Like my fans support me for cricket, I hope they will support me for dance as well. The public knows I can't dance, so I hope they will give me little bit of space because I am not a dancer,' said Sanath.[171]

In the second week of the show, themed as 'Dance Attack', Sanath surpassed all expectations yet again. But this time, he was nowhere close to the top performer. He totalled 24 points, still a manageable performance for a cricket superstar. Surprisingly, Sanath was not even close to being part of the eviction list. Much like the first week of the competition, Sanath and Madhuri had a bit of Sinhala bonding. Sanath got Madhuri onto the stage and taught her the Sri Lankan dance form, Baila, which even got the other two judges interested. For once, Sanath seemed at peace with himself as Madhuri attempted the Baila dance form on the hit Hindi song 'Twist' from the movie *Love Aaj Kal*.

---

[171]'My Legs Move on Pitch, Not Dance Floor: Sanath Jayasuriya', https://archive.mid-day.com/sports/2012/jun/150612-My-legs-move-on-pitch-not-dance-floor:-Sanath-Jayasuriya.htm, 15 June 2012.

It was in the third week that things went completely topsy-turvy. This episode was on the theme of 'Zodiac Signs'. Sanath was the lowest scorer in the episode. He polled just 19 votes from the judges and, as a result, was part of the eviction list along with Jayati. Sanath was finally evicted after the fans voted him out. Thus ended Sanath's stint as a dancer after just three weeks due to one weak performance.

Cameo of a Different Kind

While on the show, Sanath also appeared on a daily TV soap, titled *Na Bole Tum Na Maine Kuch Kaha*. The daily soap also aired on the same channel, Colors, as his dance reality show. Sanath's role was brief as he appeared as himself. But his presence played a crucial part in taking the show forward.

In the episode aired on 27 June 2012, Sanath is introduced by the show's main male protagonist, played by Kunal Karan Kapoor, to the kids of his love interest on the show, played by actress Akanksha Singh. This was almost meant to be a clincher because the son of the female lead dreamt of becoming a cricketer, and Kunal's character planned something big by taking the entire family to meet Sanath. Incidentally, Sanath was shown as being on the sets of *Jhalak Dikhhla Jaa* when the entire crew of the daily soap came to meet him.

Sanath went back from his reality show experience completely amazed at the 'tough experience', but with happy memories. 'The show is completely different from what I do in life but I enjoyed it thoroughly. The contestants are talented and hard-working. The three wonderful judges (Madhuri, Karan and Remo) were really warm towards me, especially Madhuri,' Sanath told wire agency

IANS in an interview from Sri Lanka.[172]

The forty-two-year-old even managed to attempt Bollywood's popular snake dance step. 'It was an amazing experience overall, but a tough one for me. I tried to put in a lot of hard work and enjoyed to the fullest. It was nice to learn a bit of salsa and jive. Before the show, I had never performed on a stage; am happy I could do so,' he added in that interview.[173]

---

[172]'It Was an Amazing Experience: Sanath Jayasuriya', https://www.sportskeeda.com/cricket/it-was-an-amazing-experience-sanath-jayasuriya, 14 July 2012.
[173]Ibid.

Acknowledgements

It was an idea that sprung out of nowhere, really.

I had reached out to Kapish Mehra at Rupa Publications about eight years ago when I had first moved to Dubai while working for the International Cricket Council (ICC). At that time, we brainstormed ideas for the autobiography of an eminent cricketer from the subcontinent.

Let us not name the cricketer, but it was a discussion that gathered momentum for a bit. But midway through those discussions, the said cricketer backed out and we lost track of the entire process.

In the meantime, I moved on in my career, and created new avenues for myself when I moved back to India. Just out of the blue, Rudra Sharma, who was working for Rupa Publications and had been acquainted with my work as a cricket journalist, contacted me. It was then that I suggested a few ideas for Rudra to consider.

One of the many topics I suggested included a biography on Sanath Jayasuriya. He had left many cricket fans in India battered and bruised in the period he dominated in the mid- to late 1990s.

With Sanath, it was not about the runs he scored, but the way he scored which had scarred the young cricket fans in the 1990s.

I set forth on a journey to explore the life of a man who changed Sri Lankan cricket forever. He was quite unlike any other cricketer and so it took a long time to catalogue the history.

There were some who did not feel comfortable talking about it, but there were quite of his 'victims' who very readily spoke about his impact.

I would like to express a huge gratitude to a whole host of former cricketers from across the globe. If I miss out a name, I apologize in advance. These include: Abey Kuruvilla, Aminul Islam, Bandula Warnapura, Brett Schultz, Champaka Ramanayake, Chris Pringle, Dav Whatmore, Duleep Mendis, Danny Morrison, Farveez Maharoof, Graeme Labrooy, Iqbal Sikander, Kiran More, Mark Butcher, Mike Procter, Mohammed Rafique, Mansoor Rana, Madan Lal, Mushtaq Ahmed, Nayan Mongia, Nilesh Kulkarni, Venkatpathy Raju, Salil Ankola, Saqlain Mushtaq, Sidath Wettimuny and Venkatesh Prasad. Eminent cricket administrators like Professor Ratnakar Shetty and veteran broadcaster Harsha Bhogle also provided crucial nuggets from their time with Sanath.

Veteran journalists like Vijay Lokapally of *The Hindu* and Saadi Thawfeeq from Sri Lanka were also very helpful. *Mid-Day's* Group Sports Editor Clayton Murzello was, as always, a source of vital information with his vast collection of books, periodicals and sports magazines from an era gone by.

Some others helped me with the contact details of forgotten cricketers. I must thank Bharat Sundaresan, Shahid Hashmi and Faizan Lakhani for the same. I must also thank my closest friend Faisal Shariff for pushing me at all times to write the book. It had always been our dream to collaborate on one.

Acknowledgements

I will fail in my duty if I do not acknowledge the efforts of my parents, father Narayanan and mother Usha, who did not discourage me while dreaming to pursue my dream. This book on Sanath would not have been possible if they had not let me watch him in his fully glory in the mid-1990s. Also, I would like to thank my sister, Kanchana, who bore my madness for the sport.

Finally, I would like to thank my wife, Sangeeta, for bearing with my frustrations at not cracking the code, long hours and generally being distracted through my process of putting this together.

There are quite a few more who shall remain unnamed, of their own asking, but still provided vital information to help piece together the career of the man they called 'Matara Mauler'.